CAPTURED
BY HIS HOLY
CALLING

CAPTURED
BY HIS HOLY
CALLING

2 Timothy 1:9

Who has saved us, and called us with a holy calling, not according to our works, but according to his own purpose and grace, which was given us in Christ Jesus before the world began.

GD Hausman

authorHOUSE®

AuthorHouse™ LLC
1663 Liberty Drive
Bloomington, IN 47403
www.authorhouse.com
Phone: 1-800-839-8640

Published by AuthorHouse 01/22/2014

ISBN: 978-1-4918-5292-7 (sc)
ISBN: 978-1-4918-5291-0 (e)

Library of Congress Control Number: 2014900920

Front Cover Photograph by James K Watson www.jameskwatson.com

Contents

Acknowledgement

The Bible tells us to give honor to whom honor is due, and so first of all I must acknowledge my Lord and Savior Jesus Christ. Without Him I can do nothing, I know nothing, I have nothing, and I am nothing. It was He who first put it in my heart to write this book and it was His grace that brought it to completion.

I want to thank my Uncle Allen and Aunt LaVon Erickson who were instrumental in introducing and leading me into the things pertaining to the Holy Spirit which was a major key to launching me into the will of God for my life and bringing me to where I am today.

A special conveyance, of appreciation and indebtedness to Joe and Mary Purcell, seasoned missionaries who mentored us during our first few years on the mission field. Their experience, instruction, correction, and encouragement were a vital element in our preparation for the ministry to which we have been called.

I want to extend recognition to our dear friend and co-laborer in Christ, Nola Kurber, who through the Spirit of God confirmed what the Lord had already spoken to me concerning this book thus cementing the Lord's desire in my heart and inducing its writing.

I would like to express my deep love and appreciation to my wife Marlene who consistently supported and encouraged me along the way, showing much patience during the challenging and sometimes frustrating times. Without her love and devotion this adventurous journey God has laid before me would not be possible.

Fulfilling the call of God is not accomplished all by our self. God orchestrates indispensible associations with people who in various ways contribute to helping and supporting us along the way. I could probably fill several pages of this book with people who have impacted our lives and to whom we are ever grateful. A huge thanks to all of our family and dear friends; you have helped and blessed us beyond words.

My thanks and expression of gratitude would not be complete without expressing such to my Pastor, Peter Gallardo. He has spoken into our lives on many occasions and has been a faithful pillar of support and encouragement to Marlene and me. It was Pastor Peter who afforded me the opportunity to take my first step into the ministry to which God had called me. He is and always will be, my Pastor.

To Monika Adcock a special thank you for undertaking the task of proof reading and editing this writing.

Preface

There is something phenomenal that happens when one is apprehended by God. This book has to do with the captivating power within the call of God that causes one both to will and to do of His good pleasure.

There seems to be times when God just drops something into your heart and so it was concerning the writing of this book. As I set at my desk studying one morning, I clearly sensed the Lord wanting me to write a book. Even though I knew it was the Lord, I expressed a somewhat derogative attitude toward the prospect. Frequently the Lord would bring it to my attention and each time I would dismiss it, reminding myself of my shortcomings, inabilities and insignificance.

This went on for nearly a year until one day we were state-side visiting our friends and fellow ministers Keith and Nola Kurber. As we sat around fellowshipping with one another Nola suddenly spoke up and said, "Gary, something just came up in my spirit; it has to do with you writing a book." Well, I couldn't neglect the prodding in my heart any longer, thus the birth of this writing. My heart's desire is that this book will be an encouragement to your faith in holding you committed to the call God has placed on your life.

Introduction

Romans 11:29

For God's gifts and His call are irrevocable.
He never withdraws them when once they
are given, and He does not change His mind
about those to whom He gives His grace or to
whom He sends His call.—(Amplified Bible)

I was just a youngster when I knelt beside my bed with my mother and gave my heart to Jesus Christ. Upon entering my teenage years I developed a tremendous interest in foreign missions. I sent away to every mission organization I could find soliciting information about missionary work on the foreign field. I spent hours poring over the packets that came in the mail, reading the stories, captivated by the ever intriguing pictures, dreaming of places such as Africa and South America.

Visiting missionaries were special; their stories kept me riveted to my seat, and their exhibits of pictures and artifacts were always a source of awe and curiosity generating an array of questions.

At the age of fifteen, while attending summer Bible camp, I was watching a presentation on the lives of missionaries Nate Saint, Bill Elliot, Roger Youderain, Ed McCully, and Pete Fleming, and how they gave their lives for the sake of the Gospel. They were all killed in the jungle of Ecuador by the Waorani tribe's people; the very people they were endeavoring to bring the Gospel to.

It is often difficult to adequately and sometimes impossible to describe in words experiences that are of a deep spiritual nature. Such was the case involving what happen next as I was immersed in the amazing story that was unfolding before me. I suddenly felt something pierce deep into my heart. The action seemed to be very quick, decisive, and astonishingly notable causing tears to well up in my eyes. I didn't know what it was nor could I explain it, all I knew was that something very astounding had taken place. I quickly looked around to see if any of the other kids noticed the tears I was trying to inconspicuously wipe away.

The experience was so profound and so precious that I never did share it with anyone. It wouldn't be until many years later that I would come to realize that it was at that time God planted deep in my heart His gifts and callings concerning His plan and purpose for my life.

By the time I was in my junior year of high school I had already decided what I wanted to do with my life. I wanted to become an aircraft mechanic and a pilot. While still attending high school I acquired a part time job at the local airport as a mechanics helper and also began taking flying lessons. Upon graduating high school I continued the pursuit of my dream, my plans, and entered aircraft mechanics technical school.

After graduating technical school I began my career as an aircraft mechanic. As years went by, like countless others, I slipped into the routine affairs of everyday life; a job, a wife and family.

At the age of twenty six I moved my family to Alaska and for the next fourteen years was consumed with pursuing and fulfilling my plans and my dreams. I never left church or fell into gross sin, I had married a wonderful Christian girl and we were actively involved in a local church. But little did I know at the time that the gifts and callings of God are irrevocable, and what God had deposited deep into my heart many years earlier was about to emerge and change my life forever.

Although words seem to be at times elusive and some things shared in this book are still tender and bring tears, I have endeavored with the help of the Holy Spirit to convey the radical change that takes place in one's life when God takes hold and one is truly "Captured by His Holy Calling".

It is important to realize of that God calls individuals and reveals His will in various ways. Be careful not to put God in a box by seeking someone else's experience. Seek after God and let God be God!

CHAPTER 1

A Divine Destiny

Ephesians 1:11

In him we were also chosen, having been predestined according to the plan of him who works out everything in conformity with the purpose of his will—(NIV)

THE PREDETERMINED COUNSEL OF GOD

I was always under the impression that people entered ministry because they chose to be a pastor, a missionary, or some other form of minister just as one may choose to be a doctor or lawyer. But the Word of God teaches differently and reveals that God divinely calls, supernaturally equips, and sets in position, ministers of the Gospel as it pleases Him not as it pleases man. The Bible clearly makes known that God has a specific plan and purpose for every individual. And as He states in Jeremiah, His plans and purposes are for good.

In Jeremiah 1:5, the Lord revealed to Jeremiah that before he was formed in the womb of his mother He knew him. God also told Jeremiah that before he came forth from the womb he had been sanctified, or set apart, and ordained to be a prophet unto the nations. This knowledge and wisdom of God concerning us as individuals is also spoken of in the book of Psalms.

Psalm 139:16
"You saw me before I was born. Every day of my life was recorded in your book. Every moment was laid out before a single day passed. How precious are your thoughts about me, O God! They are innumerable!"—(NLT)

Our lives are not, as many believe it to be, a life of whatever will be will be, and that our future is not for us to see. God has chosen us from before the foundation of the world that according to the predetermined counsel of His own will, in Him we should live, move, and have our being.

Many people take predestination to mean that whatever happens in your life, whether good or bad, is God's will for you and there is nothing you can do about it. An example of this kind of thinking would be; if God destined you to be saved, then you will be saved; if not, you won't. This kind of thinking is of course not in line and consistent with God's Word. Everything that happens in a person's life is not necessarily the will of God as many are led to believe.

The Bible tells us that Jesus Christ was the Lamb slain before the foundation of the world *(Rev.13:8)*. Even before God created the world, before He created man, He had already preplanned man's redemption. In other words, God had a preplanned destiny for all men.

1 Peter 3:9 says that God is not willing that *"any"* should perish, but that *"all"* should come to repentance. And in 1 Timothy 2:4 the Bible says it is God's will for *"all"* men to be saved and come to the knowledge of the truth. God has a destiny for every individual, but God has also given every man a free will, the power to make their own choices.

2 Corinthians 5:17-21 reveals that God has already [past tense] reconciled the world to himself through Jesus Christ and it is now the choice of each individual whether or not to accept and receive that work of reconciliation. God's Word explicitly states that Jesus Christ came into the world to save sinners; that Jesus Christ died for the whole world, not just a select few, and whosoever will call upon his name will be saved. Whosoever means anyone. But yet every day thousands die and go to Hell. Why? Because it's God's will for

them? No! Because of the choices they made; they choose to reject God's way of salvation.

God's predetermined plans however, go beyond the plan of redemption for mankind. They also involve His plans and purposes for us individually as born again Christians.

As I look at predestination, I see two things. First, I see "pre" which to me indicates a form of beginning. Secondly, I see "destination" indicating a specific desired end, or a specific goal that one is advancing toward.

Referring to his own life, Apostle Paul said in Acts 26:19 that he was not disobedient to the heavenly vision. This revelation was not something that Paul composed for himself, nor was it conceived in the mind of any other man. This revelation Paul received was what God had envisioned concerning His will for Paul's life. At the end of Paul's life he says, "I have fought a good fight, I have finished my course". Paul had reached God's desired end where his life was concerned. However getting to that desired end was not automatic; Paul says he was "obedient" to the call. That implies that Paul's will, not God's will, had much to do with whether or not he reached God's desired end for his life which God had predetermined for Paul just as He did for Jeremiah.

God has a new beginning for every person with a desired end. The beginning starts with accepting Jesus Christ and the desired end is the fulfilling of God's plan and purpose for each individual life according to His divine will.

I see two aspects to the will of God, the first being God's will that applies to every believer without distinction or exception. For instance; it is God's will for us all to grow in the knowledge of Jesus Christ, to be holy even as he is holy, to walk in love, to be conformed to the image of Christ, to pray, to study and meditate in His Word, to be witnesses etc., etc. This first aspect of God's will is revealed within the pages of the Word of God and at any time I can go to the Bible and discover this first aspect of God's will for my life.

The second aspect of God's will I see concerns the specific call regarding a believers God appointed place of service.

This second aspect of God's will doesn't apply to everyone equally. In other words, not everyone has the same calling *(Romans 12:4-8)*. For example, it is God's will for some to be pastors, but not everyone. The

Bible teaches that the Body of Christ consists of many members but not all members have the same function *(1 Corinthians 12:28-31).* The

The Bible also teaches that each member of the Body of Christ is closely joined and firmly knitted together, *(Ephesians 4:16),* and that we are living stones God is building into a spiritual temple *(1 Peter 2:5).*

God had a blueprint for the tabernacle that Moses built in the wilderness and He has a blueprint for His spiritual temple the Church. This blueprint contains all the specifications and details concerning the placement and function of every part which consists of every born again believer. Apostle's Paul and Peter both state that we all have been given gifts and graces for the purpose of contributing to the overall life and growth of the Body of Christ and are to be faithful in our stewardship of them.

So the specific, or individualized will of God, is that plan and purpose which God has designated for a particular individual for the purpose of fulfilling a predetermined role within the body of Christ according to His divine objective.

The general will of God, which applies to all believers without distinction, is relatively easy to know and understand because it is revealed in the Bible precept upon precept, line upon line. However, when it comes to the call of God concerning your place and function within the Body of Christ, you cannot necessarily go to the Bible and find it spelled out precept upon precept, line upon line.

God called me to go to the foreign mission field. That was God's specific will where my life was concerned. But I didn't find that in the Bible. In other words, the Bible doesn't say, "Gary you are called to be a missionary on a foreign field". Now I can find examples in the Bible of people being called by God to go to such and such a place which enables me to judge my call, but it doesn't spell out my call in black and white. We must understand that there are things that God reveals to us through His written Word the Bible, and then there are things that God reveals by speaking directly to our spirit by the Holy Spirit.

Man, though he tries to do it all the time, cannot tell you what God's specific plan for your life is. God is the only one who can do that and He does it through a direct revelation to your spirit. It is important that we don't confuse the way people under the Old Covenant were led and the way people under the New Covenant are to be led. People under the Old Covenant did not have the indwelling of the Holy Spirit; they were not born again. Therefore, whenever they needed to enquire of God about something they would go to the prophets to get answers and direction.

Under the New Covenant however, believers are not led by prophets. Under the New Covenant, all believers have the indwelling of the Holy Spirit by virtue of the new birth. Under the New Covenant, believers are to be led not by prophets, but by the Holy Spirit who lives in them.

Romans 8:14
For as many as are led by the Spirit of God,
they are the children of God.

Jesus, in referring to the New Covenant, said the Holy Spirit would teach us all things *(John 14:26)* and would guide us into all truth *(John 16:13)*.

This does not mean that God won't speak to you through a man or woman of God. The Lord may use a man or woman of God to confirm some things that He has already spoke to you or has already placed in your heart. Man didn't call and set me in ministry, God did. However, there are men and women of God that have spoken, by the Spirit of God, into my life concerning the things that God had already placed in my heart and called me to do.

Apostle Paul in speaking of his own calling says, "Paul, an apostle, not of men, neither by man, but by Jesus Christ and God the Father" *(Galatians 1:1).* In other places he says, "Paul an apostle by the will of God."

There is a difference between being called by man and being called by God. Being called by man, which includes calling yourself to a ministry, only plants the call in your mind. Being called by God plants the call in your heart, your inner most being.

There is something about God that reaches into the depths of man's heart and absolutely captures it in a way that man is unable to do. Something that is planted only in the mind is unstable, it has not become a living part of your very being and therefore when storms of adversity rise in opposition, one will quickly change their position on being in ministry.

I have never doubted the call of God on my life. It is firmly rooted deep in my heart. When times of adversity come, it is like a refuge and repels anything that would come against it. When thoughts are bombarding my mind, it is like an anchor that keeps me fixed and unmovable. When things seem to be falling out from under me, it's like a resolution that keeps me standing firm.

A call that is not planted deep in the heart does not afford that kind of security or confidence. In all the challenges I have faced where the call of God on my life was concerned, the call was my anchor. A call that is only anchored in the mind is an undependable anchor. But a call that has been planted deep in the heart is a sure anchor that will hold in times of storms because it is embedded in your inner most being.

It is from the heart that the issues of life flow *(Proverbs 4:23)*. Not only is it from the heart that the issues concerning my own personal walk with God flow, but also the issues of life concerning any ministry God may have set me in.

In God's dealings, He always goes to the heart *(spirit)* of man and it is out of the heart that the mind of man is enlightened to the things of God *(Proverbs 20:27)*. I would not have known God's plan for my life concerning ministry unless God had revealed it to me. When did the knowledge of what God wanted to do with my life come; when I sought the Lord with all my heart.

As I look back on my Christian life, I am stupefied at the number of years I was totally oblivious to the will of God where my life was concerned. I have from time to time wondered what my Christian life would have been like if I would have known earlier in life what I know now. I suppose this thought crosses the minds of many, but we can't allow ourselves to be shackled by "if I only had". I can only press forward in what I know today. I can only follow the example of Apostle Paul; *"Forgetting those things which are behind and reaching forth unto those things which are before, pressing toward the mark for the prize of the high calling of God in Christ Jesus" Philippians 3: 13-14.*

We can't change the past but we can change our future by making the right choices and daily press toward the things God has placed before us.

I don't know what God has preordained for your life, but the Bible says that God's plans for you are good!

Jeremiah 29:11
I know the plans I have for you, says the Lord. They are plans for good and not for disaster, to give you a future and a hope. (NLT)

The general will of God for your life will be found within the pages of the Bible. But the specific purpose that God has for you regarding your place within the Body of Christ will be revealed as you get on your face before God and sincerely seek Him with all of your heart.

CHAPTER 2

The Power of His Touch

Throughout the Bible we see God using diverse methods, some more dramatic than others, to get the attention of man for the purpose of fulfilling a divine objective; a burning bush, the belly of a whale, a blinding light and even through the mouth of a donkey. The method God chooses to reveal His will is not important. What is important is that we come to the knowledge of what He wishes to accomplish in and through our lives.

Because man is made in the likeness and image of God, that is, man is a spirit being just as God is a spirit, I believe that everyone has some measure of an awareness of divine purpose even though they may not understand what it is or what role it plays in their lives. People are ever searching to discover who they are and what their purpose is. They are perpetually trying to satisfy and fulfill that inner sense of purpose through all kinds of means.

Only the creator of something knows the true value and purpose of the thing created and the true plans and purposes for an individual's life can only be found in and revealed by the one who created man which is God himself.

Concerning myself, it was the power of God's touch that captured my attention. The first thing that captured my attention was the miraculous healing of my knees. The second thing was the instantaneous and dramatic effect the baptism with the Holy Spirit had on me.

If anyone were to ask me what it was that caused the most notable change in my life, I would have to say the baptism with the Holy Spirit. I was so affected by this experience that it set me on a quest to seek the face of God. I found myself devouring my Bible; I just couldn't seem to get enough of it. Night after night I would awaken at 3am and pray and worship God for hours. There were many times that the Spirit of God would come on me so strong that I would run to find a place of solitude where I could spend some time with the Lord.

It was during these intimate times with the Lord that He revealed more and more of Himself to me. The more I came to know Him the stronger His hold on my life became. Years have come and gone and I am still awakened at 3am and the Lord is still revealing things about Himself which further strengthens His hold on me.

Apostle Paul's attention was seized on the road to Damascus *(Acts 9:1-18)* and as a result, Paul took heed and sought to know and understand what it was the Lord wanted of him. As Paul begin seeking God as to why He had apprehended him, God begin to reveal His will to Paul.

Once God got my attention and I embarked on seeking Him, I then begin to receive revelation of not only God himself, but of His will where my life was concerned.

Fulfilling the call of God is following a path of progressive revelation. God will make the first move, but then He waits for a response. God will not make a person respond to Him. Such an act on the part of God would violate the free will that God gave man and He will not violate a man's choice.

God appeared to Moses in a burning bush but didn't make Moses turn aside to see the sight. But as soon as God did see that Moses, of his own free will, turned to give attention to the burning bush, God spoke to Moses concerning what He was calling him to do. As Moses walked in obedience, God gave him further revelation concerning things he was to do involving leading the children of Israel.

God didn't "make" me become a minister of the Gospel. He didn't "make" me go to the foreign mission field. No, the power of His touch had so captured me that I was willing to do for Him whatever He asked of me. When we turn toward the beckoning of God, He then begins to speak, and revelation of His plans and purposes come forth.

God called me to preach and teach His Word. However, the call to minister God's Word can carry a variety of meaning such as in what capacity, where, to whom, and when. Those questions were answered as I sought God and walked step by step in faith and obedience to what He had told me to do.

When we accept the call, God then opens to us further revelation pertaining to the fulfilling of that call. Each proceeding revelation is given as one obediently walks in the previous revelation. If one refuses to obey what God is saying to do, then no further revelation is given.

In the natural realm we walk step by step and if we fail to take a step, our walk comes to a halt. It is the same in walking with God in His plans and purposes for our lives. It is step by step, and failing to take the next step brings our walk in God's plan to a halt.

God's will concerning His call on my life was and still is a progressive revelation. The Bible says we go from faith to faith and from glory to glory. In fulfilling the plan of God for our lives, we progress from revelation to revelation, each revelation requiring greater faith than the previous which results in a greater glory than before. In speaking of the glory in the Old Testament, it referred to the manifestation of God, a manifestation of His presence. Today I am walking in a greater revelation at a higher level of faith than ever. As a result of this, I am experiencing greater manifestations of the glory of God in ministry as well as in my personal life.

It is human nature to want all the answers and details before hand, but then, that wouldn't require any faith and our life is a life of faith, including our ministries. There are times when it would seem easier if I knew all the details before hand. But as I look back on some of the things God has asked me to do, I am glad I didn't know everything up front. Had I known some of the details involved with what God was asking me to do before hand I probably would have drawn back.

God wants us to accept and obey based not on our knowledge of the details, but based on the knowledge of who He is. Who is He? FAITHFUL!

"FAITHFULL IS HE THAT CALLS
YOU, WHO WILL ALSO DO IT"

CHAPTER 3

Knowledge of the Truth

Mark 4:33

And with many such parables He spoke the word to them as they were able to hear it.

It is God's will that we all come to the knowledge of the truth. But for various reasons, many times we are not ready to hear or accept the truth.

Jesus spoke the word to people only to the degree they were able to hear it. Apostle Paul also refers to times when he could not talk about certain things not because he didn't want to, but because the people were not at the point of receiving it in the sense of ascribing it value.

I was no different when it came to things pertaining to the Holy Spirit. When the Pentecostal view of the Holy Spirit was brought into discussion I wasn't in the place of hearing and therefore took no account of it, placed no value on it at the time and so brushed it aside. One reason I was so brutish in this area was because I thought I already knew everything there was to know on the subject and that my views were right. The problem was my views were not formed by the truth of the Word of God but by what I was taught by others. Apostle Paul in 1 Corinthians 8:2 says, *"If anyone thinks that he knows anything, he knows nothing yet as he ought to know."* I knew some things about the Holy Spirit, but I didn't know those things as I ought to have known them. The subject of the Holy Spirit wasn't the only area in which I thought I knew all that was needed to be known, but there were also several other things I didn't know as I ought to have known.

It all started for me during a visit with my Aunt LaVon and Uncle Allen Erickson. I have always been close to my aunt and uncle and I love them dearly. I wouldn't be where I am today if God hadn't brought their influence into my life.

I moved from Minnesota to Alaska in the spring of 1977 and on my way I stopped to see them. They had made a move to Montana some years earlier and I hadn't seen them for quite some time. They didn't know I was coming and were quite surprised to see me and it nearly blew them away when I told them I was on my way to Alaska. As we visited, it wasn't long before it became very obvious that things in their lives had changed drastically since the last time I saw them.

Like me they had spent most of their Christian life in a traditional church, but now after being gloriously led into the baptism of the Holy Spirit they were attending a full gospel church and growing in the things of God. Allen tried talking to me about the things God had done and was doing in their lives but I was not really interested in hearing about it. After spending a few days with them I bid them goodbye and resumed my journey to Alaska. It would be several years before I would see them again.

In December of 1984, we loaded up our Ford Bronco and headed down the Alaska Highway to spend Christmas with family whom we hadn't seen since our move to Alaska in 1977. LaVon and Allen drove from their home in Montana to spend Christmas Day at my parent's house in Minnesota and we only had a brief time together. Before they left to return home they asked us to stop and see them on our way back to Alaska and so before heading back up the Alaska Highway, we stopped in Montana to visit them.

We had a good time together, catching up on the past several years and I was quite surprised and even more aware of the change in them. During our time together LaVon and Allen would try to inject a little here and there about the Holy Spirit, but again, I wasn't ready to hear. All I really knew about the Holy Spirit was that he was the third person of the God-Head. I certainly didn't know anything about the working of the Holy Spirit in and through a person's life. If someone had asked me why Jesus sent the Holy Spirit, I wouldn't have had clue. Boy, you talk about being ignorant. I was as dumb as a post.

Let me take a moment right here to throw in another thought. As I look back at this particular time, I realize that LaVon and Allen never tried to force things concerning the Holy Spirit down my throat so to speak. They perceived that I was not at the place of hearing and held their peace. The wisdom of God says there is a time to be silent and a time to speak. There are numerous accounts of people who have been driven away from the truth because wisdom wasn't used in presenting the truth. The Bible points out that even though we know the truth in a matter, we can do harm to others with our knowledge if it is not applied with wisdom. I thank God for LaVon and Allen's wisdom for it left the door open for the time to come when I was ready to hear. Oh that we would learn to walk in the wisdom of God!

Well, they could see I wasn't ready and so we talked about other things. We talked a lot about Alaska and Allen seemed quite interested. After spending several days with them, we headed back to Alaska and went on with life as usual. Several months later they contacted us and said they were being led to move to Alaska.

To this day, I believe with all my heart that it was the divine providence of God not only for them, but especially for me. I hadn't the vaguest idea of the impact their moving to Alaska would have in helping bring me to a crucial pivotal point in my life.

After their move to Fairbanks, they began attending a local Charismatic church and sometime later opened their home to a weekly Bible study. They of course invited us to come and after some prodding I consented to attend. At first I was a bit apprehensive and felt out of place because first of all, it wasn't like any Bible study I was use to attending. I begin to hear things that were quite contrary to what I had been taught to believe and the first thing I came face to face with was my attitude. Anyone who has done any gardening knows that the process of preparing the ground for a productive crop requires time and effort and is not always a pleasant chore. Such was the case with me when my wife and I began attending this Bible study.

In the parable of the sower, Jesus reveals to us that it is possible for us to hear and yet not hear. I believe that most people can probably relate to this. How many times has someone been talking to you and when they are finished you have no idea of what they just said even though you heard them speaking. This is a common problem in marriages, especially on the part of the husband. Even though you were hearing words being spoken, you weren't hearing with the intent of hearing to comprehend or understand what was being said. It all has to with desires, attitudes, and the value you place on who is doing the talking and on what is being said.

Jesus on more than one occasion said, "He who has ears to hear, let him hear." Four times in chapters 2 & 3 of Revelation, Jesus says, "He that has an ear let him hear what the Spirit says." This is where we miss it so many times; we hear but we don't hear. The Bible reveals two important aspects related to hearing: 1) what you hear, and 2) how you hear. "WHAT" you hear has to do with your desires and "HOW" you hear has to do with your attitude.

In Mark 4:24, Jesus said, "Take heed what you hear." This phrase "take heed" implies turning your eyes to something and giving it your undivided attention with the intent of gaining understanding in an absolute sense with the purpose of capitalizing on what is being attended to. What we have in life and what we don't have; where we are and where we are not in life, are directly related to what we take heed to listening to.

Jesus' remarks in Mark 4:24 address the issues of faith. Faith is simply a persuasion, a conviction or system of beliefs one has embraced asserting that a certain thing is true and therefore worthy of their trust resulting in corresponding actions.

Luke 8:18 says, "Take heed how you hear." How you hear has to do with ones attitude toward what is being heard; in this case the Word of God.

The whole parable of the sower *(Matthew 13:3-23, Mark 4:1-32, Luke 8:5-18)* exemplifies a person's attitude toward God's Word and the direct effect attitude has upon the Words ability to bring forth fruit.

The manner in which I hear, or give attention to the Word of God, reveals the true value I place on what God says and is directly related to my faith. How I treat the Word of God, how I respond to it, how aggressively I attend to it, will determine the magnitude of what the Word of God produces where my life is concerned.

On one occasion, just before I was to take the pulpit to minister on the subject of healing, the Lord brought to my attention Luke 5:15. The Lord said that the people came to hear with the intention of being healed. He said these people had already heard of him by word of mouth. News of him had spread throughout their region and when they heard that he had come to their region, they didn't come just to hear a good message but came with a specific purpose, to hear *"and"* be healed.

People hear, but their hearing many times carries no purpose. This is where many miss out on the blessings of God and forfeit the grace that could be theirs and this is exactly what was happening concerning my own life.

God is always endeavoring to bring us revelation of his will and of himself. He desires to take us beyond just an intellectual knowledge of him. God's aspiration is to see the blessings of His promises manifested in the lives of his children bringing them into an experiential knowledge of Him. But as Jesus implies in Mark 4:24; this can only happen to the degree that one is willing to hear with the intent of procuring the benefits of what is heard.

Romans 10:17 says that faith comes by hearing and hearing by the Word of God. For my faith, my convictions, my system of beliefs to be based upon genuine truth, I had to put aside all my preconceived ideas and the doctrines of man that I had been taught, and "HEAR" the Word of God.

If I am to receive the revelation that God desires me to have and walk in all that He has called me to, I must always have the ground of my heart prepared with the attitude of hearing with intent.

I was hearing about divine healing, the gifts of the Spirit, the baptism of the Holy Spirit and speaking in tongues. I was hearing about walking by faith, living by faith, being led by and walking in the Spirit. Never had I heard such things. I thank God for my Christian parents and godly upbringing. I thank God for the Sunday school teachers, Pastors, and spiritual leaders that had positive influences on my life while growing up. But there were certain truths that were either never mentioned, or not taught according to what the Bible says concerning them.

Healing was something that happened only because God choose to make your case special.

Speaking in tongues of course was of the devil and you best stay away from those kinds of people. The gifts of the Spirit had been done away with and were not for today. Faith was simply a word that identified you as being born again and as such, now a person of the Christian Faith. Because of this previous teaching, as well as some of my own preconceived ideas which were established upon what I heard others say, I had a hard time accepting what I was hearing in this Bible study.

It was like a war zone. In my spirit I would feel a sense of aspiration, a pricking in my heart, like a lighthouse emitting rays of hope to a floundering ship in the darkness. But then in rebuttal my mind would revert back to the old system of beliefs that I had adopted and quench the arousal in my heart; healing is not for today, tongues is of the devil, the gifts of the Spirit ceased when the last apostle died etc, etc, etc. But in spite of the constant battle I was experiencing, something kept drawing me back to this Bible study week after week.

After several weeks the conflict seemed to ease a bit and I begin to see from the Word of God the credibility and proof of what I was hearing. I realized that the arguments I previously had concerning such matters were not with those who were teaching them, but with the Word of God itself. The Word of God confronts, it cuts deep, discloses and lays bare all leaving nothing hidden *(Hebrews 4:12).*

In my own eyes I considered myself to be in pretty good shape. But the Word revealed unyielding, calloused, and fallow ground. It revealed hard places where I had absolutely refused to accept truth. It unveiled stones causing shallowness in my Christian faith and divulged thorns that were thwarting the will of God where my life was concerned. I undoubtedly had lots of serious gardening to do.

I realize now of course that it was the Holy Spirit in me revealing not only the truth of the Word of God, but also revealing to me the true condition of myself, bringing conviction and prodding my heart to believe. The Bible says that it is God's desire that all men come to the knowledge of the truth. Jesus refers to the Holy Spirit as the Spirit of truth *(John 16:13)* and that one of His jobs is to guide us into all truth. Not just a portion or half truth, "ALL" truth. The Holy Spirit dwells in us and He is always endeavoring to bring us into the whole truth. The Bible also tells us that the Spirit and the Word are one. The Holy Spirit will always witness to the truth, the Word of God. He will always move in line and be in agreement with the Word.

Romans 8:16 tells us that the Holy Spirit bears witness with our spirit. What does the Holy Spirit witness to—the TRUTH. The Holy Spirit is the Spirit of truth and will always bear witness to the truth. The Bible also tells us that the Holy Spirit who dwells in us yearns jealously *(James 4:5)*. Another translation of James 4:5 says the Holy Spirit fiercely desires. What does the Holy Spirit jealously yearn for, what does he so fiercely desire? He yearns and desires to teach us all things and guide us into all truth!

Proverbs 20:27 says that the spirit of man is the candle of the Lord. That means that God will lead us and guide us through our spirit. If we would learn to listen to our spirit rather than our head, the Holy Spirit who dwells in us and bears witness with our spirit, would lead us right into the truth just like Jesus said He would in John 16:13. But many times we are listening to our own reasoning and are hindered often by the doctrines and traditions of man. This was a big part of my problem. I never learned to be spirit led; I never developed any kind of relationship with the Holy Spirit. My whole life was governed by and revolved around my own reasoning and physical senses.

Mark 7:13 clearly shows that many times the reason the Word of God doesn't work in people's lives as it ought is because of tradition. Apostle Paul also testifies to the fact that the cross of Christ, the Gospel, is made of no effect through the wisdom of mans words *(1 Corinthians 1:17 & 2:4-5)*. Wisdom simply means to be skillful at something and there are those who are very skillful in explaining away the truth of the Word of God, rendering it powerless not only in their own lives but in the lives of their hearers. The Bible says, *"Let God be true, but every man a liar"*

I found it to be to my advantage to follow the example of the Berean's who received the word with readiness of mind *(Acts 17:11),* and of the Thessalonica's who received the word not as the word of men, but as it is in truth the word of God *(1 Thessalonians 2:13).*

For years I listened to sermons and teachings without ever checking them out for myself against the Word of God. Brother Kenneth Hagin said something that has always stuck with me. He said many Christians are like baby birds; their eyes are closed but their mouths are wide open ready to swallow whatever comes along. Jesus told us to take heed to what we hear. We are not to swallow just any thing we hear hook line and sinker. Some of what I had been taught was truth, some was half truth, and some was not truth at all.

The Bible tells me to trust in the Lord with all of my heart and to lean not on my own understanding. There were many questions that I had to come face to face with. Do I trust in the leading of the Holy Spirit? Do I trust in the Word of God? Am I willing to trust in the Lord and allow Him to lead and direct me into the truth which Jesus said would make me free? Or, am I going to trust in my own judgment, my own reasoning, my own understanding, and follow my head instead of my heart?

It is important to understand and accept the fact that there is only one truth; God's Word is Truth *(John 17:17)*. God does not say one thing but mean another. This was the great deception that caused the fall of man in Genesis chapter three; "Yes, God said . . . but He really didn't mean what he said . . . what He really meant was . . ." In other words, the devil always perverts and twists the Word of God trying to get people to believe something that it does not really say.

WHAT GOD SAYS GOD PRECISELY MEANS

Numbers 23:19
God is not a man that he should lie, nor the son
of man that he should change his mind:

Psalm 89:34
My covenant will I not break, nor alter the
thing that is gone out of my lips.

God means exactly what He says and will never go back on His word. The Bible says that His promises are steadfast and sure because when he made promise, he swore by Himself.

In my case, for God to impart revelation of the truth to me, I had to come to the place where I would listen without any reservations to what God was saying. Psalm 119:130 says that the entrance of God's Word gives light (revelation); it gives understanding to the simple. Well, I certainly was a simple one. Thank God for His Word and the light it brings!

Once I begin dealing with my attitude, and begin to really listen, it wasn't long before I was experiencing the reality of the truths I was seeing in the Word of God concerning these seemingly controversial teachings. Jesus said when we know the truth the truth will make us free. Free of what? Free of whatever is binding us; and erroneous teaching is bondage.

One day as I was sharing with a friend concerning what had taken place in my life and all the wonderful things that were happening, I was bluntly told that I had been "Brain Washed." These kinds of remarks have all the potential of leaving one offended. But instead of becoming offended, I started laughing on the inside of me. I was laughing on the inside of me because my friend was actually right and I had to agree with what he said.

In Romans 12:2 we are instructed not to be conformed to this world, but to be transformed by the renewing of our minds.

That word *"transformed"* in Romans 12:2 is the Greek word *"metamorphoo"* from which we get our English word metamorphose. It means to go through a process of becoming completely different. It signifies to be changed into something you were not before. The transformation of a caterpillar into a butterfly is called the process of metamorphose and is a good example of this word "be transformed."

My mind had been transformed, completely changed from its previous condition. In other words, my old way of thinking was transformed, washed away. I began thinking in line with the truth of God's

Word. As a result of a transformation of mind, my whole way of life was transformed. So in a sense, I had been brain washed—by the Word of God!

A change of thinking causes a change in believing which causes a change of action which in turn causes a change of life!

CHAPTER 4

Jesus My Healer

Exodus 15:26

I am the Lord that heals you

One controversial point of doctrine that has plagued the Body of Christ is that of divine healing for the physical body. Collisions over doctrine and questions concerning physical healing in the Atonement of Christ have produced discord and division in the Church. Many teach that Jesus healed in order to prove His divinity. Some teach God replaced divine healing with medical science and that it certainly isn't God's will to heal everybody. Erroneous teachings like this have kept many in bondage to sickness and disease.

During my years in high school, I was a participant in the gymnastics program and in the process of mastering the sport I had severely damaged my knees. My knee joints became so loose that any kind of twisting or irregular movement would invariably cause dislocation and the task of forcing them back into place was extremely painful. I was scheduled to have surgery performed on them a few months after graduating high school but my application to attend aviation technical school had been accepted and so I canceled the operation.

I never did have them operated on and over the 19 years that followed, my knees became increasingly worse and made even walking any distance a painful event. To this day, just thinking about it, and even now while writing this, I grit my teeth because the feeling that comes with forcing a dislocated knee back into place is something you never forget.

THE POWER OF LIES KEEPS PEOPLE IN BONDAGE
THE POWER OF TRUTH SETS PEOPLE FREE

My wife and I had been attending a home Bible study being hosted by my Uncle Allen and Aunt LaVon and for several months heard much about divine healing. During this time I had read and studied all the accounts of healing in the Bible and listened to personal testimonies of others who were wonderfully healed by the power of God.

At the close of one of the meetings, an invitation was given for anyone who wanted prayer for healing and I now found myself face to face with the opportunity to prove the Word of God to be true where my life was concerned. I spoke up and said yes, I would like prayer for my knees.

Allen then laid his hands on my knees and commanded them to be healed in the Name of Jesus. I sensed a warm sensation spread over my knees as Allen prayed, but other than that I felt nothing out of the ordinary.

Now this was a new experience for me because in the traditional churches in which I was raised, I don't ever remember anyone laying hands on people for healing and certainly never heard anyone command healing.

Later that night as I lay in bed thinking about all the things that took place earlier that evening, my knees embarked on a major pain campaign. Not only did they hurt, but I could feel them throbbing just like a finger does when it has been smashed with a hammer. They were painfully pulsating to the point where if I could have watched them as I lay there in the dark, I believe I could have seen them literally moving in and out with each palpitation. I had lived many years with these knees and never in all those years had the pain been so intense. The first thought that ran through my mind was, "What did these people do to me?" After several hours I finally drifted off to sleep, my knees still throbbing with pain.

The next morning, my wife having already left the house, I got up and went into the kitchen to fix some breakfast. As I was walking back and forth across the kitchen fixing my breakfast I realized that something was different but couldn't put my finger on it. I went on with preparing my breakfast still sensing that something was different.

On one of my trips across the kitchen I suddenly stopped dead in my tracks as I finally realized what it was. Standing there, right in the middle of the kitchen, I dropped my pants to the floor and stared in amazement at my knees. For years, standing with my toes pointed straight ahead, my knee caps would stare directly at one another. But on this morning, standing there with my toes pointed straight ahead, both of my knee caps were pointing the same direction as my toes; straight ahead!

All that day in absolute amazement I put my knees through every kind of test I could think of to try to dislocate them but nothing worked. I twisted, turned, jumped and run but nothing affected them. God had completely and totally healed my knees! Since that time they have never caused me any pain, I can walk for miles without any problems, and they have never again dislocated.

The Lord has healed me on several occasions of various things simply through my faith, but in the spring 1992 I again experienced the miraculous healing power of God in my life in a special way.

I have always enjoyed riding motorcycles, especially dirt bikes. Even after I was married, riding dirt bikes was one of my favorite hobbies. In the summer of 1976, I was out riding with my friends as usual. On this particular day we had stopped to play on a short but relatively steep hill. While climbing the hill we would practice doing wheelies, and it was actually quite fun.

On one of my runs I inadvertently let the bike get behind its power curve and it began to bog down. As I was playing with the throttle trying to keep the bike in a wheelie there came a sudden burst of power and the bike jumped up and over on its left side leaving my left foot firmly planted on the terra firma on the down side of the hill with my right leg over the still ascending bike.

Because the hill was so steep and the bike in such a precarious position, I couldn't get free of the bike. With my left leg going nowhere and my right leg still traveling with the bike, I experienced excruciating pain as my groin muscles disengaged from active duty.

I rolled down the hill and lay on the ground in agonizing pain and of course my friends all gathered around laughing and joking about my crash. After about ten minutes the pain seemed to subside and I was able to get up. I actually didn't feel all that bad so I got back on my bike and played around for another hour before deciding to head for home.

After arriving home I discovered that I couldn't move my legs to get off the bike. Every time I would try, I would feel nothing but intense pain. Since it was obvious that I was not going to be able to dismount the bike without assistance, I called out to my wife Marlene. She came to the door and asked me what I wanted and I told her I couldn't lift either one of my legs to get off the bike and I needed assistance. She put her hands on her hips, which is usually a sign from her that I am in some kind of trouble, and asked "What did you do?" Well, bless her heart, she helped me off the bike and into the house and sat me down on the sofa.

The pain now had become a constant throbbing and a sharp pain would run through my groin every time I would try to move my legs apart. Marlene asked me if I needed to go to the doctor, but you know us guy's; I said, "No, I'll be just fine"! But the longer I sat there the stiffer my groin became and greater the pain when I tried to move. Finally late that evening I succumbed to my wife's prodding and she took me to the hospital emergency room.

I was taken to the x-ray room and stretched out on the table. The doctor then asked me to spread my legs apart so they could get a good x-ray. My immediate reply was, "If I could spread my legs, I wouldn't be here"! The x-ray revealed that the groin muscles had been torn away from the pelvis; not good! Anyone who has ever had a groin injury knows that it takes quite some time for that type of an injury to heal and in my case the rips were severe and never seemed to completely heal.

After a couple of months I went back to riding my bike and everything was fine until it was time to get off the bike. I discovered that after 30 minutes of riding I couldn't lift my legs to get off without experiencing intense pain. Well, this ended my bike riding days and throughout the following years my groin caused me problems, especially in walking for extended periods of time or in situations that required any extensive spreading of the legs.

In spring of 1992 while I was attending RHEMA Bible Training Center, my mom and dad came to visit us. Before the end of their visit we took them to the Tulsa Zoo and spent a good part of the day walking around the zoo. By the time we were ready to leave, my groin had become so stiff and painful that it made it very difficult to walk. We got to my dad's truck and he asked me to drive. His truck had a manual transmission and just operating the clutch was painful.

Now I had been working at RHEMA while attending Bible school and at that time my work hours happen to be from 4pm to 9pm. Since school was from 8am to 12 noon, this worked out great, because it enabled me to attend prayer and healing school in the afternoon before going to work. I had been attending healing school not because I needed healing, but because I wanted to learn more about healing. God had miraculously healed my knees and I had a hunger to know more.

Well, mom and dad left the day after our trip to the zoo and I'm back in school Monday morning. My groin was a little stiff, could feel some pain, but it wasn't particularly giving me trouble. After my last class I went to prayer school and then to healing school as usual. On this particular day, the teaching was out of the Gospel of John regarding the healing of the Nobleman's son and how the man simply believed the word that Jesus spoke to him concerning his son and went his way.

I always sat in the back of the room because like I said, I wasn't there for healing, I was there to learn. As I listened to the teaching I wasn't conscience of or thinking about my groin but was simply soaking in the truths of taking God at his word. After the teaching was over, we all stood up and entered into a time of worship. As I stood there with my hands raised, worshiping and thanking God for His word, for His promises and the teaching that I had heard, I felt as though I was standing under a warm liquid, not being poured over me, but through me. It started at the top of my head, went down through my entire body and out my feet. Now I had experienced the tangible anointing of God many times prior, but not quite like this.

Well, the class ended and I went to my job at the campus gym. As I was working that evening, I realized that I wasn't experiencing any stiffness or pain in my groin. As I did with my knees, I began to check things out and a primary telltale test would be to spread my legs apart as far as I could. I stretched and stretched and stretched; no pain, no stiffness. I then went upstairs and run three laps around the running track. Wow! No pain, no stiffness, I had been healed and have never experienced any trouble with my groin since!

Someone may ask, "Well, why didn't God heal your groin the same time He healed your knees?" Well, at that time my groin wasn't troubling me and I wasn't seeking healing for my groin, I was seeking healing for my knees.

Whether you choose to believe or not to believe, God's Word remains the same and just like Him, it never changes. Just because some choose not to believe does not nullify the Word of God where your personal life is concerned.

In speaking of divine healing, many people will say, "Yes, but what about so and so, they were prayed for and never got healed" and they will tell you all about some person's experience in not getting healed. Healing is not about someone else's experience, not even mine. It's all about what God says on the matter and what you chose to believe and act on.

YOU SHALL KNOW THE TRUTH AND THE TRUTH SHALL MAKE YOU FREE

In John 8:32 Jesus said, *"You will know the truth and the truth will set you free"*. But He qualifies this statement in verse 31; *"If you continue in my word"*.

After I got filled with the Holy Spirit I started fellowshipping around full Gospel people and I would often hear "You will know the truth and the truth will set you free". I heard it so often from preachers that I thought it was some kind of cliché that full gospel people used. I found out of course that it was actually in the Bible.

Well I was new in all this and was ignorant of a lot of things. But as time went on, even I could see that even though people knew the truth they were not free. This baffled me until the Lord pointed out verse 31 of John chapter 8. He said people are not set free simply by knowing the truth. They are set free as they take the truth they know and habitually apply it in their lives.

Proverbs 4:20-27 and Proverbs 6:20-23 gives a clear implication of what Jesus is saying. If you will do His word, if you will practice His word, not draw away from it and not let it depart from you, then the truth will have power in your life.

I have discovered two factors concerning God's truth where my own life is concerned. First, God's truth, which is His Word, will have no effect in my life unless I do the truth. Secondly, I will never have a working knowledge of God's Word until I apply the Word and allow it to prove itself true.

It is important to have an intellectual knowledge of God's Word, but we must also have a working knowledge of God's Word. One thing I have learned that is vital to knowing and understanding the truth is this; unless I do the truth the truth will never prove itself true where my own life is concerned. When referring to doing the truth, I am referring to "application" of the truth.

Just having knowledge of the truth is not enough. There are thousands who have heard the message of salvation. They have knowledge of it but are still unsaved, they are still lost in the sense that they are not born again. Why? Because they have not done what is necessary to make the truth of eternal life a reality where their personal life is concerned. They haven't done what Romans 10:9-10 says to do; "believe and confess Jesus Christ as Lord and receive him as such".

Just knowing what the Bible says about salvation won't save you. It's the personal application of it that makes salvation a reality in a person's life. I would never have been healed if I hadn't acted on the Word of God.

The same principle applies to any truth in the Word of God. One can have knowledge of it but unless one personally takes that truth and by faith applies it to one's own life, the Word can never prove itself as truth where their life is concerned.

Many have knowledge of healing, yet healing is not a reality in their life. I can hear preaching and teaching on it, I can hear about it working in someone else's life. I may even witness it happening in someone else's life, but it will never work in my own life until I by faith personally apply it to my own life.

James tells us to be doers of the Word and not hearers only *(James 1:22)*. He goes on to say that faith without action, or application, is dead being alone *(James 2:17, 26)*. When any truth in the Word is applied, it must be applied through faith.

Unless I believe the Word of God to be truth as Jesus said it is *(John 17:17)* and act upon it, I will never experience the reality of it in my own personal life. James says it's the doer of the Word who is blessed. It is the doer of the Word who receives the blessing of the Word.

Believing is a choice, it's a decision. Each individual must make their own choice concerning the question of whether the Bible really means what it says or whether it means something other than what it says.

When I made the decision, when I made the choice to believe and yield to God's Word, it proved itself to be true by producing in my life what it said it would, which in this case was healing.

The Bible says that God watches over His Word to "perform" it. And faith is the spiritual law that God has set over the releasing of the power in His Word where our lives are concerned.

TRUST ME

Faith is a demonstrated trust in God and I am reminded of another instance of healing.

Back in 1997 I had a situation where my back had slipped out of place right between my shoulder blades. It was hard to work and almost impossible to get a good night's sleep. Even just sitting upright in a chair wasn't comfortable at all. I had prayed over it and it seemed like nothing was happening.

After three days with no relief, I decided that if it wasn't gone by lunch time the next day I was going to a chiropractor for help. Well, the next day came and still no relief. I went to work, noon came and no change.

I walked out to my car to go find a chiropractor and as I opened the door to get in the car, from inside of me I heard these two words; "Trust me." Well, I had become well acquainted with the Lord's voice and I knew immediately that it was the Lord speaking to me. Tears weld up in my eyes and I said, "Ok Lord" and I closed the car door and went back to work.

Two more days passed by and still no change in my back. I knew I had heard from God on the matter and so I just kept saying, "Lord I trust you, you told me to trust you so I'm going to trust you." The next day I went to work feeling no different, but again told the Lord I trusted Him. At some point in time during that day while I was working, I couldn't even tell you when, I suddenly realized that the pain was gone and my back was completely normal.

If we look at the Bible from beginning to end, there is really only one thing that God is asking of us; "Hear what I say and trust me." After all, that's what faith in God is all about; hearing and trusting. If people would dare to believe the Word of God for what it is, the truth, and by faith apply it to their lives; God would confirm His Word by manifesting forth the power of His Word proving it to be true and setting people free in many areas of life including their physical bodies.

I am absolutely and fully persuaded concerning God's will when it comes to divine healing. I have seen healing not only in my own life, but in the lives of countless others that we have ministered to. I have seen God's Word confirmed too many times to believe otherwise.

God loved and cared enough about me to heal me. That captured me and now compels me to lay hands on the sick and see them healed. What a wonderful thing it is to let God minister His truth to you, capture you by it, and then use you to minister it to others by the power of the Holy Spirit for His glory!

The message of Christ the healer has been firmly planted and established in my heart. He is the healer!

Take God, take Him at His word, allow Him to minister His truth to your heart, not your head, your heart, and be captured by the fulfillment of His Word in your own personal life.

Let God's word prove itself in your life. Faith for healing begins with believing that He is Jehovah Rapha, the Lord your healer.

CHAPTER 5

Endowed With Power

Acts 1:8

But you shall receive power after that the Holy Ghost is come upon you; and you shall be witnesses unto Me . . .

Another truth that the Lord brought me revelation knowledge of is that concerning the baptism of the Holy Spirit with the evidence of speaking with other tongues.

The same night my knees were prayed for, hands were laid on me to receive the baptism with the Holy Spirit. Acts 19:6 says, *"And when Paul had laid his hands upon them, the Holy Ghost came upon them and they spoke with other tongues and prophesied".* Just like those we read about in the book of Acts, as hands were laid on me to receive this baptism with the Holy Spirit, the Holy Spirit came upon me and I spoke with other tongues as the Spirit gave me utterance. This event radically changed my life forever.

If someone were to ask me what it was that changed the course of my life so drastically, I would without hesitancy, attribute it to this experience of being baptized with the Holy Spirit. I am convinced that I would not be where I am today doing what I am doing had it not been for this endowment of power with the evidence of speaking in other tongues.

The baptism with the Holy Spirit has been a source of great controversy among many Christians. It is sad that the true purpose of this endowment has been veiled in the shadow of "tongues". When the subject of the baptism in the Holy Spirit is brought up it is always "tongues" that seems to be the focal point, causing strife and division in the Body of Christ. I don't believe Jesus ever meant for this to be. His purpose was to empower the Church to carry on the works that He began.

This particular subject matter was difficult at first for me to accept because for me, as it is with so many other Christians, the issue was not so much being endued with power, but the issue was speaking in tongues.

I was raised among those who didn't believe in the baptism with the Holy Spirit as an experience subsequent to the new Birth. I was taught that when you were born again you received all the Holy Spirit there was to receive and speaking in tongues was actually of the devil. As a result of this kind of teaching engrained in my mind, I struggled with this for quite some time and at times even coming to the point of anger. I believe the Lord saw my frustration and the struggle I was having with my own thoughts and I thank God He showed me the truth.

WHEN HE THE SPIRIT OF TRUTH IS COME HE SHALL GUIDE YOU INTO ALL TRUTH

Jesus said one of the purposes for which the Holy Spirit was sent, was to teach us all things and guide us into all truth *(John 14:26; 16:13).* This is a tremendous promise given to us which sadly is too often neglected and disregarded.

In Matthew 7:7-8 Jesus makes this promise; *"Ask, and it shall be given you; seek and you shall find; knock, and it shall be opened unto you: For every one that asketh receiveth; and he that seeketh findeth; and to him that knocketh, it shall be opened".* And so I begin to ask, seek and knock concerning answers to my questions and the Holy Spirit begin to teach me from the scriptures and guide me into the truth of what I was seeking.

The scripture the Lord led me to is one that I have elated to in another chapter of this book concerning the call of God. This passage has become an indispensable reminder to me regarding whether or not God's Word to me will prosper and accomplish its purpose where my life and ministry are concerned.

I was first led to Isaiah 55:8-9 which says, *"For my thoughts are not your thoughts, neither are your ways my ways, saith the Lord. For as the heavens are higher than the earth, so are my ways higher than your ways, and my thoughts than your thoughts".*

From this scripture in Isaiah, the Lord showed me that His way of thinking is not my way of thinking and that His way of doing things is not my way of doing things. It was revealed to me that I was trying to line the Word of God up with my way thinking, with my own reasoning. I was trying to line up God's Word with the traditional teaching that I had received and it was causing confusion and frustration.

The Lord then showed me how to solve my problem in Isaiah 55:7—*Let the wicked forsake his way, and the unrighteous man his thoughts: and let him return unto the LORD, and he will have mercy upon him; and to our God, for he will abundantly pardon".*

My problem was not letting go of my own way of thinking. The Lord showed me that if I would align my thoughts with His thoughts instead of trying to align His thoughts with my thoughts, His Word would produce in my life what it says and I would experience the promise given in Isaiah 55:10-11—*"For as the rain cometh down, and the snow from heaven, and returneth not thither, but watereth the earth, and maketh it bring forth and bud, that it may give seed to the sower, and bread to the eater: So shall my word be that goeth forth out of my mouth: it shall not return unto me void, but it shall accomplish that which I please, and it shall prosper in the thing whereto I sent it".*

An understanding of the Word of God, which is spiritual, cannot be achieved through the natural mind. Apostle Paul says that the natural mind is hostile toward God and cannot receive the things of the Spirit of God. That is why Apostle Paul and Peter speak of being renewed in our mind; in other words, in our thinking. I had to line my thinking up with God's thinking and the first step involved in doing that was changing my attitude.

I finally made the decision to change my attitude and told my mind to shut up and listen to what the Bible, which is God's thoughts and ways, actually had to say on the matter. I begin to search the scriptures concerning this subject of receiving the Holy Spirit. As I begin to compare what I had been taught with what the Bible actually said, I discovered that some of the things I had been taught did not line up with the Bible.

The second step involved with aligning myself with God was taking captive and laying aside thoughts and traditions that were contrary to what the Bible actually said and humbly acknowledge the Bible not as the word of man but as the Word of God.

Jesus in addressing the Pharisee's, said that because of their traditions, they rendered the Word of God powerless. By hanging on to our traditions we can render the Word of God ineffective where our lives are concerned. Understand that not all traditions are bad, there are traditions that we want to keep. However, traditions that obstruct people from experiencing the fullness of what God has for them and impedes what God's Word is able to accomplish and produce in their lives are traditions we do not want to keep.

When I lined myself up in agreement with the Word of God, I received what the Word said I would receive; I received the baptism with the Holy Spirit and power with the evidence of speaking in other tongues.

There are those who argue that when you are born again you receive all the Holy Spirit there is to receive. But, did we receive all the Holy Spirit there is to receive when we got saved? Because of previous teaching, this was a question that I myself had to have answered. And again, the Holy Spirit led me to the truth which is the Word of God and answered that question for me.

In John 20:22 we see the disciples "receiving" the Holy Spirit, but yet 40 days later, Jesus told them to remain in Jerusalem and "wait" for the promise of the Father which was the baptism with the Holy Spirit *(Acts 1:2-9)*. If the disciples received the Holy Spirit in John 20:22, which was before Jesus ascended into heaven where He is now seated at the right hand of the Father, then why did Jesus instruct them to remain in Jerusalem and wait for the Holy Spirit which came after He ascended into heaven? The answer is because there was something more involving the Holy Spirit that Jesus wanted his disciples to receive.

What the disciples received in John 20:22 was the new birth, the "indwelling" of the Holy Spirit. What they received on the day of Pentecost was an "endowment of power", the Holy Spirit upon them to enable them to preach the gospel in power and demonstration of the Spirit. In other words, they were empowered to carry on and do the same works that Jesus did which was preaching and teaching about kingdom of God with signs and wonders, such as healing the sick, casting out demons, and raising the dead following.

Receiving the new birth is the work of the Holy Spirit in us, making us a new creation in Christ, imparting to us the gift of eternal life. This work of the Holy Spirit in us continues throughout our life helping in the developing of our personal daily walk with God. It is the well of water within us *(John 14:14).*

Although there are some personal benefits that come from being baptized with the Holy Spirit, receiving the baptism with the Holy Spirit is primarily the power of the Holy Spirit working through us for the purpose of witnessing or ministering to the needs of others not in word only but in power. In other words, it is not power for living, but power for serving. It is the river of living water flowing out of us *(John 7:37-39).*

There were several things I experienced after receiving this baptism in the Holy Spirit. The first thing I experienced was an incredible hunger for the

Word of God. I found myself literally devouring the Word. I couldn't seem to get enough of it. The Word of God became a living thing to me as God brought forth revelation after revelation of scripture. I was seeing things I had never seen before. Scriptures I had known and read for years seemed to jump off the pages of my Bible in a new and living way. I spent hour upon hour in my Bible devouring every word. This illumination of scripture caused an even greater hunger to know more.

The second thing I experienced was the intense desire to pray, especially in other tongues. There would be times while at work I would find myself looking for a place to pray, even if it was just for a couple of minutes. The urgency to pray left me feeling like it was a matter of life and death. I could hardly wait to get home from work so I could get alone with the Word and pray.

The third thing was that I acquired an acute awareness of the voice and presence of God that I never had before. What Jesus said in John chapter 10 regarding His sheep hearing and knowing his voice became a reality. God talked to me about things I had no idea that he was interested in or even cared about concerning my life.

The fourth thing I experienced was a loss of desire for other things. By loss I simply mean my desire for other things just disappeared. I cannot tell you where they went, I can only say that they were not there anymore. I searched for them but could not find them. I loved and lived for hunting and fishing, but all that disappeared. I had other aspirations, but they also vanished away. It is like they became shadows in the light of my desire for what God was doing in my life.

I also began to experience several manifestations of the gifts of the Spirit. The word of knowledge, the gift of prophecy, the discerning of spirits, and the gifts of healing as revealed in 1 Corinthians chapter 12 begin operating in my life. At the time I had no understanding of these things and it wasn't until Bible school that I understood what was happening and the purposes and intensions of these manifestations. I learned these things were a part of the anointing God had placed on my life.

Acts 10:38 say's. *"How God anointed Jesus with the Holy Spirit and power, who went about doing good and healing all who were oppressed of the devil for God was with him".*

This same anointing that God empowered Jesus with empowers us for service today. I would not want to be in ministry without the empowerment that this anointing brings. I thank God for the anointing that not only works within me, but also works through me. This endowment of power has become very precious to me for I have seen what it does as it touches the lives of others and sets them free. I endeavor to do whatever is necessary to protect it because I would never want to lose my anointing.

What is this anointing that empowers us? Well, Jesus said in Luke 4:18, "The Spirit of the Lord is <u>UPON</u> me because He has <u>ANOINTED</u> me to preach the gospel . . . And so that anointing is the Spirit UPON us. The same Spirit and power that God anointed Jesus with, He also anoints His servants with today for the same purpose.

THAT'S WONDERFUL BROTHER GARY, BUT WHAT ABOUT THE TONGUES?

Well, the Bible is very clear; tongues "is the evidence" of receiving this endowment. How did the disciples discern whether or not people received the baptism with the Holy Spirit? The Bible says "they heard them speak with other tongues" just as they did in the beginning. We do not however, receive the baptism with the Holy Spirit just so we can speak in tongues.

Jesus didn't tell the disciples to wait for the Holy Spirit so they could speak in tongues. No, Jesus told them to wait in Jerusalem UNTIL they were ENDUED WITH POWER *(Luke24:49)*. The disciples weren't waiting for the experience of speaking in tongues; they were waiting to be endowed with power.

We receive the baptism with the Holy Spirit for the purpose of being divinely empowered to be a witness of Jesus Christ. The Bible says that the kingdom of God is not in word only, but in power and in demonstration of the Spirit *(Mark 16:17-20, Acts 4:33, Romans 15:19, 1 Corinthians 2:4; 4:20, 1 Thessalonians 1:5)*.

Being a witness of Jesus Christ goes beyond just telling someone about Jesus. It is also a demonstration of the resurrection power of Christ and a manifestation of the redemption that he purchased with His own blood.

Speaking in tongues is a part of this divine empowerment package which enables us to pray on a supernatural level apart from and far above our own natural understanding.

I KNOW HOW TO PRAY, WHY
DO I NEED TONGUES?

Someone said to me, "I know how to pray, so why do I need tongues to pray?" I might note that this is one of the questions I had myself. Well, thank God we do know how to pray, but what does the Bible really say about praying. 1 Corinthians 14:14-15 say's, *"for if I pray in a tongue, my spirit prays but my understanding is unfruitful."* Verse 15—*"What is the conclusion then? I will pray with the spirit, and I will also pray with the understanding."* The understanding that Paul is referring to is what we understand with our natural mind. In other words, the knowledge we have acquired through our own natural intellect.

When praying with my own understanding, which is praying in my known language of English, my prayer is limited by my own natural mind, in other words, by how much of the English language I know. When praying with my own understanding, I cannot pray beyond what I know, I cannot pray beyond what I can express in my own native language. It is very easy to run out of words to say and exhaust my knowledge of the English language when in prayer. This only leaves me feeling helpless and unsatisfied.

There is more I would like to say, there is more in my heart, but don't have the words to express it. However the Holy Spirit is not limited by our understanding, He is not limited by our native languages.

The Holy Spirit knows the perfect will of God and He knows what is in the heart and mind of God. He possesses all the knowledge and wisdom of God. Praying in other tongues is the supernatural assistance that the Holy Spirit gives us in praying beyond our own understanding the perfect will of God in any matter *(Romans 8:26-27).*

When praying with our own understanding, prayers can often become contaminated with words that are spoken out of our feelings and emotions. They can also be contaminated with words spoken out of the doubt and unbelief that is coursing through thoughts. This is what was happening in the account I am about to share with you concerning a situation I was praying about with my own understanding. In other words, I was praying in English. In the process of praying, I mixed in all my feelings, emotions, some doubt and unbelief and none of these things accomplish anything in prayer.

Praying in other tongues keeps my prayer pure and free from contamination which otherwise can render my prayer powerless. Does this mean then that prayer is not to have any emotions or feelings involved with it? NO, I did not say that. What I am saying is that sometimes people allow their feelings and emotions to govern their prayer. Our feelings and emotions have their place even in prayer, but they are not to be the governing or controlling factor in how we pray.

SPEAK YOUR OWN LANGUAGE!

I felt it a great honor to be asked by veteran missionaries Joe and Mary Purcell to join their ministry team in Russia, and our three years with them has proved invaluable many times over.

Well, I had been sensing in my heart for several months that there was some kind of change coming our way but I would dismiss it and try not to think about it. Change is not something that is always welcomed with open arms.

After our third year of working with these wonderful missionaries, I was informed that invitations for a new visa would not be available for the following year. I was assured that it was not a matter of rejection but one of promotion.

Even though for nearly a year I had been sensing a change coming in our ministry, the feeling that came with such news was one not of promotion, but one of rejection.

Thoughts begin to fill my mind, thoughts of failure, thoughts of not being good enough, and of not doing a good enough job. Devastated by the news I begin to beat myself up with reproach and was on the verge of giving up and quitting ministry altogether. Everything seemed to be falling apart. Promotion?— Promotion to what? I couldn't see anything in front of us. All of these things were rushing in like a herd of stampeding buffalo and I felt trampled under the weight of total despair. Then gently, but oh so powerfully, the vision and words of Jesus rose up inside me, "Remember Lot's wife and don't look back".

I immediately began to cry out to God, my only plea being, "Lord, I just want to be in your will". And through my weeping and crying out I heard these words, "You are in my will".

I told the Lord that invitations back to Russia were not going to be issued and asked what I was supposed to do. I felt utterly helpless in the situation but the words that came to me next jolted me out of my pity party and brought me to my senses. When I had asked the Lord what I was supposed to do, he said in a very stern way, "SPEAK YOUR OWN LANGUAGE"!

Well I knew exactly what He was referring to. Rather than blubbering over my situation, voicing my doubts, speaking negatively, and filling my prayer with all my feelings and emotions, I was to start praying in other tongues. In other words, I was to start speaking the language that God had given me in the baptism of the Holy Spirit for the purpose of praying things out according to His perfect will.

I immediately begin praying in other tongues and after awhile the grace and peace of God descended on me filling my stricken heart with peace and joy. It wasn't long and the Lord opened the door to our next phase of ministry. We were back in Russia with new invitations, new visas and in a new place of ministry. PROMOTION! Thank God for utterance in other tongues; our own personal God-given prayer language!

I learned a very important lesson from this experience. I learned not to ignore the stirrings in my heart but to take those things and begin to pray them out in other tongues. The Lord told me that everything concerning my life and ministry would be birthed in prayer, maintained in prayer and brought to fruition through prayer. You see if I would have done this when I first sensed this stirring in my heart concerning change coming, I would have avoided all of that stress, frustration, and anxiety I went through.

This is only one example in my own life of hundreds that I could give involving the value of praying in tongues. There is much more I could say on this subject, but the focus of the book is not speaking in tongues so I will move on. I will however in closing say this; I believe with all my heart that it was this kind of prayer, praying in other tongues, that helped me get to the place I am today and is the kind of praying that will continue to help me fulfill and finish my God given task here on earth.

THANK GOD FOR UTTERANCE
IN OTHER TONGUES!

CHAPTER 6

Pursuing the Call

Philippians 3:7-8

But those things which were profit to me, I gave up for Christ. Yes truly, and I am ready to give up all things for the knowledge of Christ Jesus my Lord, which is more than all: for whom I have undergone the loss of all things, and to me they are less than nothing, so that I may have Christ as my reward.

One of the reasons for moving to Alaska, besides the job opportunities, was the hunting and fishing. My dad taught me how to hunt and fish when I was very young and I have always enjoyed it and even more so after moving to Alaska. I lived for hunting and fishing and the long daylight hours made for ideal after work pleasure.

Many times after working all day I would load up the airplane and fly out to my favorite fishing spot for an evening of enjoyment, returning well after midnight with plenty of daylight to spare. There was hardly a weekend went by that I wasn't either out fishing or hunting. But God had moved on my life in such a powerful and profound way that those desires just left. My desires and priorities had changed. My only desire was to serve God and to know him more. I had been "Captured by His Holy calling".

Embedded in the call of God is a power that holds an undeniable sway over one's life (if it is allowed to). It is an apprehension that will at times motivate one even beyond their own understanding and more often than not completely surpasses the understanding of others. This is the place that I call "bitter-sweet". Bitter in the sense of having to undergo the reviling of people who don't understand and sweet in the sense that you know you have heard from God and are in His will. There is a price to be paid in the wake of pursuing the call of God, a price that I had never really associated with yielding oneself to the will of God.

Often when counting the cost we take into consideration the more obvious things, like leaving the security of a well paying job with all its benefits, letting go of a nice home with all its comforts and laying aside other material possessions. But one thing that is often overlooked is the price that one may have to pay relating to relationships with family and friends.

The cost is not so much in possibly having to leave them in order to do what God has called you to do, although it can be painful, but the price to be paid often comes in their attitude and response to your obeying God. This is an especially high cost when it involves your family and longtime friends who are Christians. I found this to be the most painful part of answering the call of God and following Jesus Christ. You can be well assured that not everyone will share your exuberant enthusiasm and excitement over God's plan for your life.

I have heard it all: stupid, crazy, off the edge, brainwashed, disillusioned, you're making a big mistake, etc, etc. Accusations were even made that I was going through a mid-life crisis which was causing me to think and act irrationally. I was accused of throwing away a 30 plus year career and wasting my education and talents. People's intentions are often sincere and at times even sound rational, but only from a natural human standpoint.

The call of God is not of the natural man and therefore cannot be understood or rationalized by the natural man. The Bible says the natural man does not receive the things of the Spirit of God for they are foolishness to him, nor can he know them because they are spiritually discerned.

The call of God was never meant to pacify the flesh or appease man's reasoning. Many things that God calls us to do are not pleasing to the flesh, are contrary to human reasoning and are at times seemingly foolish.

The call of God on an individual's life can come in various ways, but regardless of how, it is the "Word" of the Lord coming unto you saying do this, do that, go here, go there. And so the call of God is a "Word" that comes forth from the mouth of God to an individual.

Isaiah 55:11 tells us that the "Word" which God sends forth out of His mouth will not return to Him void but will accomplish that which He pleases and will prosper in the thing whereto He sends it. Well, we can jump and shout over this, however, we must look at how this "word" that comes to us materializes. If we look at the previous verses in this passage of scripture, it is reveled to us how this "word" of the Lord that comes to us is consummated and becomes fruitful and prosperous.

Verses 9-10 of Isaiah 55 reveals that God's thoughts are not our thoughts neither are our ways His ways. In verse 7 He tells us to forsake "our" ways and "our" thoughts and turn to Him. In other words, turn to His thoughts and His ways.

Any thought or way I may have, or someone else may have, that is contrary to God's thoughts or God's ways where my life is concerned is wrong and I must make a choice. The Bible says, "There is a way which seems right to a man, but the end thereof are the ways of death" *(Proverbs 14:12)*. No matter how right it may seem to me or anyone else, it doesn't necessarily make it the right way.

When Jesus was talking to His disciples about the things concerning his crucifixion, Peter through the influence of Satan tried to get him to take an alternate route. The Bible instructs us not to let any man beguile us with enticing words. The devil will always try through enticing words, to get us to take the easy way, the less painful and less costly way. The call of God is often discarded because of family, friends and even worldly possessions and pleasures.

The choice is always ours. God will not force anyone to follow after Him. I must choose whether to follow my own or someone else's thoughts and ways, or like Jesus, turn to the Lord and keep Him always before my face. I must stay in that place where He makes His ways known to me, where I always hear His voice and know His thoughts that I not be moved *(Acts 2:22-28).*

Genesis 24:27

As for me, going on the way of obedience and faith, the Lord led me. *(Amplified Bible)*

As long as I keep my eyes on Jesus and go the way of obedience and faith, God will lead me and promises to see that the call on my life, the "word" that He sent unto me, will be fruitful, prosperous, perfected and brought to fruition.

I have been scourged up one side and down the other for going to the mission field. "Surely there's something you can do in the U. S. Surely there's a church here in the States where you can fulfill God's call; why go to a foreign country? You need to be close to your family". Perhaps you have heard these same things. It is imperative that we don't allow those things to move us away from the word of the Lord that has come to us saying.

During our second year on the mission field in Russia, due to expiring visas, we made a trip into China so we could re-enter Russia thereby activating our new visas. We were gone for about seven days and returned to Russia on Christmas Eve. The next day, which was Christmas Day, we received an email that Marlene's mother had passed away.

Marlene was very close to her mother and although we were aware of her mother's health, this news was very hard on Marlene. Especially being thousands of miles away and not being able to be there. We were not in the United States where you could just jump on a plane any time you needed to. There were no daily flights out of where we were and Marlene of course was unable to be there for her mother's funeral.

There were those who thought this was absolutely unpardonable and therefore worthy of their cynicism. What they didn't know is what took place several months earlier when we delayed our return to Russia so that Marlene could make a special trip to the lower 48 just for the purpose of seeing her mom who had just been hospitalized.

Being held at a distance by loved ones as a result of answering the call of God, whether they be friends or family, has been to me the greatest cost and deepest source of pain. I believe Peter got a glimpse of this pain in the eyes of Jesus the night he held Jesus at a distance and betrayed him. Assuredly Apostle Paul experienced this pain, as time after time brothers in Christ abandoned him.

I am reminded of a story I once heard about a small boy who was getting ready to go to bed during a severe thunderstorm. The little boy was frightened and as his father tucked him into bed the little boy said, "Daddy, could you lay down with me, I'm scared". The father tried to comfort and encourage his son by telling him he had nothing to fear because God promised that he would always be with us. The little boy looked up at his father and said, "I know dad, but I need someone in skin".

Thank God that He is always with us, that He will never leave us or forsake us. We can draw comfort and strength from His promises. But even though God is always there to help us, it's also nice to have someone in skin that will help encourage us in our pursuit of God and His plan for our life.

The magnitude of the price one may pay in responding to the call of God is found in allowing oneself to be captured by the Holy Calling of God. This simply means forsaking whatever needs forsaking, doing whatever is necessary, and embracing the grace of God.

The call of God always places us above what we ourselves are capable of doing and demands strength and stamina that only the grace of God can give. But as long as I stay in the way of faith and obedience, I can be sure of always being in the right place at the right time doing the right thing.

Through the years I have learned that if I am going to follow the call of God on my life, not everyone is going to understand, not everyone is going to agree and rejoice with me. This is not only true in the initial obedience to the call of God, but also true many times relating to transitions that come in ministry. There is a saying that goes like this; you can please some of the people some of the time, but you can't please all of the people all of the time.

God has moved me into different roles of ministry which often required a change of location. I discovered that even on the mission field, although it is God who is moving you, there are those who consider you a traitor for leaving their city, leaving their church and going somewhere else. I thank God for family members who do stand by us and for those precious people in skin that God has divinely placed around us to be an encouragement and support in our pursuit of the call of God.

Count the cost! The call, along with the anointing and grace to fulfill that call, are a gift. But even though it is freely bestowed upon us, saying "yes" to the call of God does carry a price. The bottom line in pursuing the call is this; you must love Him more than anything or anybody else. It is this level of love for the things of God that will compel you in your pursuit of the call of God on your life.

CHAPTER 7

You Must Be Mistaken!

Amos 7:14-15

I was no prophet, nor was I a son of a prophet, but I was a herdsman and a tender of sycamore fruit. Then the Lord took me as I followed the flock, and the Lord said to me, 'Go, prophesy to my people Israel.

Throughout the Bible we see men called of God to accomplish great things, who in the eyes of man and in their own estimation were not qualified.

Gideon was a man called of God to deliver Israel from the hands of the Midianites. But Gideon saw himself as a man from the weakest tribe of Manasseh, the least important member of his family and therefore on considered himself not qualified.

Jeremiah was called and ordained to be a prophet unto the nations. But when God approached him he said, "Ah, Lord God! Behold, I cannot speak for I am a child".

And then there was Moses, a man called to deliver the children of Israel out of the bondage of Egypt. He said, "Who am I that I should go unto Pharaoh, and that I should bri ng forth the children of Israel out of Egypt?" Moses went on to say, "O my Lord, I am not eloquent, but I am slow of speech, and of a slow tongue".

From God's response to each of them, we can clearly see that God, without any consideration of man's deficiencies or self-imposed limitations, chooses those through whom He desires to accomplish His plans and purposes. What God chooses to accomplish through a man or woman is not bound by their inadequacies nor is it limited to their natural capabilities. The call of God, and the achievement of such, is based upon who He is and His sufficiency. Apostle Paul say's it is God who makes us able ministers of the Gospel.

We all have shortcomings and weaknesses leaving us feeling inadequate, inept and incompetent just like Gideon, Jeremiah, or Moses. But the great lesson we see here in the call of these great men is that God doesn't call the qualified, He qualifies the called. God doesn't make mistakes; He makes mighty men and women of valor!

My initial response to God regarding preaching wasn't much different. As I had already shared, one of the things I experienced after the baptism with the Holy Spirit was an intense desire to pray, especially in other tongues. As I was lying on the floor praying one evening, the longer I prayed the stronger and more intense the prayer became. After a considerable period of time went by, I saw something approaching from a long way off. The closer it came the bigger it got until finally, right in front of my eyes were the words "Preach My Word."

I believe what happens many times when God calls someone, is that instead of looking at the call from God's view point it is looked at from the natural stand point. In other words we don't consider who God is, God's ability, what He has and what He can do. Instead we look at who we are, what we have, what we can do, and from this view point there will always be a sense of incompetence.

Throughout scripture we can see a common denominator God used concerning those He calls. When God calls He ever tries to impart vision. He wants us to see things as He sees them. When God called Moses to deliver the children of Israel from Egypt He tried to get Moses to see himself as God was seeing him. But Moses only saw his natural inabilities and used them as an excuse to try to disqualify himself from the call of God.

Another example is that of Gideon. When the Angel of the Lord approached Gideon He said, "THE LORD IS WITH YOU, YOU MIGHTY MAN OF VALOR"—"GO IN THIS MIGHT OF YOURS AND YOU SHALL SAVE ISRAEL FROM THE HAND OF THE MIDIANITES." Gideon was hiding in fear of the Midianites and his response was much like Moses. Gideon judged his ability to accomplish what God was asking him to do, not in the light of God, but in the light of himself.

God's vision of Jeremiah was a prophet to the nations, but Jeremiah's vision of himself was that of a child. God told him not to say he was a child. Not seeing ourselves as God sees us and talking about ourselves contrary to what God says about us will impede ones stepping into the call of God. God always sees us not according to who or what we are in and of ourselves or even how we perceive ourselves to be, but He views us in light of who He is and what He is capable of doing in and through us. If God can use the mouth of a donkey to speak through, surely he can use anyone.

LORD, YOU MUST BE MISTAKEN!

When the Lord called me to preach, my reaction was, "Lord you must be mistaken"! My perspective and arguments were based exclusively on the guise of the natural side of things, not even taking God into consideration. I knew what I was, and in my eyes I certainly wasn't preaching material. I knew what my limitations were and standing up in front of a bunch of people to preach was definitely outside the boundaries of my comfort zone.

I would nearly die of heart failure every time I was asked to read a simple portion of scripture in front of the congregation. With heart beats approaching redline, breathing all of a sudden became laborious and at times even painful producing irregularities in my voice and speech. This of course generated an acute awareness of myself causing my hands to begin shaking and released torrents of sweat. I knew that public speaking was definitely not my forte. But all of these impediments, no matter how insurmountable they seemed to me, had no influence on the determinate counsel of God's will where my life was concerned.

I had never before preached, neither was I ever asked to preach. But just a few days after this vision of "Preach My Word", doors began to just amazingly open for me to preach. I was well versed in my inabilities and thoroughly acquainted with my experiences with public speaking and I could have flatly refused God's call. But I had been captured by His Holy Calling and my only desire was to do His will and not disappoint Him.

I distinctly remember the first time I took the pulpit to preach, it was if as I were someone else. I experienced no nervousness, no butterflies, no shaking, sweating or anxiety, just a peace that at that time I did not understand. As I opened my mouth to speak, the words seemed to just flow out without any effort at all. At that point in my life I knew virtually nothing about the gifting and callings of God. I of course now know that it was God's grace and His anointing that comes with the call that was at work enabling me to preach.

Many who have been called are waiting on God for the anointing *(really what they are waiting for is a feeling of some sort)* before they will obey the call. Although the anointing is tangible at times, the anointing is not a feeling. The anointing is God's ability to fulfill God given tasks. It wasn't feeling the anointing to preach that caused me to step out and start preaching. Back then I didn't know anything about the anointing; I didn't even know I had an anointing. No, it was the love of God that had so unequivocally captured me that caused me to step out and do what God told me to do.

God calls us to repentance and salvation because He loves "us". But he calls us to serve, not because He loves "us", but because He loves "those" whom He is sending us to. I believe this was the love that constrained Apostle Paul to preach the gospel.

It wasn't until after I stepped out in obedience to God that I noticed something apart from myself was at work each time I ministered. Sometime later I came to the understanding that it was the anointing and grace that was manifesting, enabling me to do what God told me to do. There have been numerous times before a meeting, even though I prepared myself with the Word and prayer, that I felt absolutely nothing. I felt just as dry and empty as could be. But as I began to minister, God would meet me every time with His grace and anointing.

OBEDIENCE OF FAITH RELEASES
THE ANOINTING

If God has called you, the anointing is there. But the anointing to do what God called you to do will not manifest until you step out in faith in obedience to the call. When the children of Israel were ready to cross the Jordan River and enter the promise land, the Ark of the Covenant which represented the presence and power of God, was with them. But the Jordan River didn't part until the priests carrying the Ark obeyed God's instructions and stepped into the water.

The anointing manifests through you for a purpose. If you never by faith step into that purpose, the anointing has no reason to manifest through you. This is why those who are waiting until they "feel" anointed before they will do what God told them to do will never do it. You will never experience the anointing or the grace for fulfilling the call of God until there is that step of obedience into the call.

There is preparation time such as prayer and waiting on God that are essential to enhancing the anointing, but they will not bring the anointing into manifestation. Faith and obedience brings the anointing of God on your life into manifestation where it can accomplish that for which God has anointed you.

If you are called to preach and never preach, that preaching anointing will never manifest, it's just that simple. In my natural self, I am very quiet and reserved; that's Gary. When I am not preaching or teaching the Word of God, I am just Gary. But, when I am preaching, teaching or even just talking about the things of God, the anointing comes on me and changes Gary into another person so to speak.

Contrary to what some may believe, it is not all up to God. There is a "God side" regarding the call of God which involves the things that God is responsible for. But there is also a "man side" to the call of God which involves the things man is responsible for. It is important to understand that problems are never with the God side but always with the man side.

Apostle Paul tells us in Ephesians 5:18 not to be unwise but understand what the will of the Lord is. It is every believer's responsibility to seek out and understand what the will of God is for their individual lives. It is every believer's responsibility to pursue the fulfilling of that will. When we are faithful to do our part, God is faithful to do His.

I didn't know that God had a special plan for my life. I didn't know there was such a thing as the will of God for an individual. I always thought that people went into ministry simply because they choose to be pastors, missionaries, or some other form of minister. I always believed that ministry was a vocation that people chose and prepared for just like any other vocation. But the Bible once again corrected my erroneous thinking. God does not have a "Career Day" where he exhibits all His different ministry gifts, gives an expository on each one, lets you review them and choose which ever one you want. It is God himself who divinely calls, supernaturally equips, and sets in position ministers of the Gospel as it pleases Him.

We can doubt and second guess ourselves, but let's not doubt and second guess God. Faithful is He that called us!

CHAPTER 8

What's Rhema?

As a young teenager I had often thought of attending Bible school, and now at the age of 42 a stirring rose up in my heart concerning that very thing.

I had been praying for several months, primarily in other tongues, and I noticed one particular word that kept coming up in my prayer language; the word "rhema". I had no idea what this word meant, but every time I prayed this word would come up over and over. Each time this word came out of my lips it was unmistakably distinct, would jump up in my spirit and invariably catch my attention. I would momentarily stop and ponder over why this word seemed to be so notable and what its significance was.

One day I mentioned my desire to go to Bible school to my Uncle Allen. He asked me if I had ever thought of going to RHEMA. As soon as he mentioned the word rhema, something on the inside of me clicked and I asked, "What is rhema"? He told me it was a

Bible training center in Tulsa, Oklahoma that was started by Kenneth Hagin. I didn't know anything about RHEMA or Kenneth Hagin, but the Lord quickly brought to my attention that this is what had been coming up in my prayers for the past several months and this is where He wanted me to go to Bible school.

AND HE SENT THEM OUT TWO BY TWO

Amos 3:3
Can two walk together unless they be in agreement?

This scripture in Amos 3:3 is a most important truth that must be taken into account regarding husbands and wives when it comes to fulltime ministry. I learned this lesson very early in my call to enter the ministry.

My wife and I had already been married for nearly 20 years when God begin drawing me toward the ministry. We were two born again Christians who had entered into a covenant of marriage. There are numerous accounts of Christian's who have divorced their spouse and destroyed their families in the process of entering ministry. Many try to justify their actions by saying God told them to do it. If I interpret scripture correctly, I don't see any evidence of God being in the business tearing apart and destroying Christian families.

After praying and establishing in my own heart that attending RHEMA was what God wanted me to do, I decided it was time to tell my wife. So one evening I asked her what she thought about moving to Tulsa, Oklahoma and going to Bible School. She thought for a moment and said, "What about my stuff"? Well, I didn't say anything, I just left it at that and took the matter to God in prayer. While I was praying about it I had a vision. I seen Marlene dressed in her favorite winter coat wearing a backpack. On the backpack was stacked all of her stuff. It was a huge heavy load and she was bowed under the weight of it.

I understood the implication of the vision, but didn't know exactly how to properly pray about it. Fortunately I did know someone who did—thank God for the Holy Spirit and utterance in other tongues! I took this vision and asked the Holy Spirit to give me utterance to pray concerning this situation. I am so glad the Holy Spirit knows what and how we should pray when we don't *(Romans 8:26-27)*.

Several days later as I was sitting on our sofa, Marlene came and sat down next to me and said,

"You know what, I can get rid of my stuff"! God had prepared my heart to go, but my wife's heart also needed to be prepared and that was something that only God could do.

The Bible says that a house divided will not stand. Within a marriage where there is a divine call to ministry, the husband and wife must be in agreement or the ministry will not be able to stand. My wife was not called to preach or teach yet she is crucial to the operation and success of the ministry which God has set me in. I did not coerce or force my wife's decision. I simply prayed and let the Holy Spirit do His work in her own heart. There have been instances where a wife was made to go against her will and as a result there was no commitment to the work, and ministry for the husband became a burden rather than a joy. Pray and let God work out the details in the heart of your spouse to be the help mate God called them to be.

Now that we were in agreement concerning the direction the Lord was taking us, it was time to begin preparing for our move. Part of this preparation involved our daughter Becki who was just two years away from graduating high school. Normally this wouldn't pose much of a problem as children are quite resilient to change. But Becki was only two years from graduating, had many friends and was actively involved in many of the school activities and programs. We knew that this would not be easy for her and that God would have to do some preparatory work in her heart also.

When we told her about our move she was sad, and it was clear that the news of our moving at this point in her life was upsetting. Well, we committed her to the Lord and held her up and supported her with our prayers. As a result, just as God worked in the heart of Marlene, God also worked in the heart of our daughter Becki. Within a couple of weeks God had done His preparatory work and she was ready and excited to make the move.

EVEN SOME GOOD THINGS ARE NOT NECESSARILY THE WILL OF GOD

Most of my life I thought all there was to being a Christian was getting saved, going to church, and as a figure of speech, keeping your nose clean. But I came to the place where I realized that there was much more to the Christian life; there was this thing called the call of God.

As we were making plans to go to Bible school I began fussing about selling our house. The house was not finished yet and the real estate market at that time was not doing well. We had only a few months before Bible school started and were pressed to get things sold so we could be on our way. Anyway, while I was praying about the house, (actually I was more complaining to God about it than praying about it), I heard Him say very clearly, "Don't sell the house, give it away, it was not my will for you to have in the first place". Those words really stunned me—no, not the words "give the house away", but the words "It was not my will for you to have it in the first place".

All these years I had been doing what I thought every good Christian is to do. I was doing good things, but it was brought to my attention that even some good things are not necessarily the will of God where our life is concerned. I suddenly realized that it is possible go through life out of the will of God without even realizing it. Owning a house is not a bad thing, it's a good thing, but this house was not God's will for us. Well, we sold everything except the house which we did give away as the Lord had instructed.

It is often hard to explain to people why you are doing what you are doing. When we give the house away, there were those who thought it was a crazy irresponsible act. But there is just something about knowing that you know that you know that causes you to do what often to human reasoning seems foolish. When you have been captured by the holy calling of God you will do things that are contrary to human reasoning and often beyond even our own understanding.

We caught a lot of flak over the fact that we were getting rid of everything we had without knowing first that I had actually been accepted by RHEMA. I had gotten the application and all the required recommendations sent in but hadn't yet received anything stating whether I had been accepted or not. Some were saying we were being premature in selling everything off and giving the house away. But I knew without a doubt that this is what God wanted us to do and that everything was fine. Right up to the moment we were loading our truck for the 4,000 plus mile trip down the Alaska Highway, I still had heard nothing from RHEMA.

The day of our departure had arrived and still no notification. So to bring some peace of mind to those who were so concerned, I made a quick call to the RHEMA admissions office. They informed me that my application had been approved, but hadn't yet sent out my acceptance letter. I told them to hold the letter because we would be there in a couple of weeks.

Often we have no idea where God is taking us or what His purpose is when He gets us there. I didn't know where Bible school was going to lead us. I only knew that the Lord said "Go". But as the Word instructs us, we are to trust in the Lord with all our heart and lean not on our own understanding, but in all our ways acknowledge him and he will direct our paths. Thank God that even when we don't understand, we can have peace and rest in knowing that he does understand and is directing our way accordingly. Over the years, one portion of scripture I have come to lean much on is Psalms 32:8 which says, *"I will instruct you and teach you in the way you shall go: I will guide you with my eye".* This promise of God has brought peace and assurance to me many a time.

After arriving in Tulsa, securing an apartment and getting settled into Bible school, it was now time to start thinking about a part time job. The Lord had blessed Marlene with a job just a few days after our arrival in Tulsa but as for me I had not yet looked for work.

I had over 30 years experience as an aircraft mechanic and so I figured I would just go to the airport and apply for a job. This seemed like an excellent idea to me; after all, I would be going to Bible school and making fairly good money at the same time. So after school one day I headed out to the airport to see about a job.

As I was zipping down the highway, totally engrossed in thought concerning my wonderful plan, something totally unexpected happened. All of a sudden I heard the words "Don't go to the airport"! The Lord has spoken to me many times, sometimes audibly, and I knew this was the Lord. But this time it was not only audible but the tone of His voice was very loud, firm and explicit. It was so loud, distinct and unexpected that it startled me and I barely had time to quickly turn onto an exit ramp that I was just approaching.

My heart had taken off like a Thoroughbred out of the starting gate. I got the truck under control and after bringing to a halt at the bottom of the exit ramp I collected myself and said to the Lord; "Well, what am I suppose to do, I've got to work to help support my family". The Lord spoke again but this time in a more gentle subdued way. He said, "Go to RHEMA and get an application".

I began to argue with the Lord and said, "Lord, do you know how many students and other people have submitted applications for employment at RHEMA"? The Lord quietly but yet very firmly said. "Go to RHEMA and get an application". I have learned that when the Lord tells me to do something, he will not listen to excuses or argue the point.

The next day after school I went and picked up an application, filled it out that afternoon and submitted it the following day. A couple of days later I received a call from RHEMA requesting an interview with one of the department heads. After the interview they thanked me for coming and I left not knowing about a job. A few days later I received another call requesting another interview.

Upon entering the administration building for my second interview, I was escorted to a small room where I was seated and told that someone would be with me shortly. I was expecting to probably meet with the same person who interviewed me the first time but to my astonishment in walked Mrs. Lynette Hagin. I was a little nervous to begin with but now I was really nervous! We had only been at RHEMA a few months and never before in my entire life had I been around people of such notoriety which I suppose was the cause of much of my nervousness.

One of the questions on the employment application was; "Why do you want to work at RHEMA". I struggled with this question as I was filling out the application several days earlier because the only thing I knew was what the Lord told me. It wasn't my idea to work there in the first place and the Lord didn't give me any reasons why I was to work there. I did however decide that I couldn't put, "The Lord told me to work here", they would probably think, "Right, we've heard that before". So after all of my reasoning, I answered the question with something that sounded what I thought would be intelligent and wouldn't raise any eyebrows.

Mrs. Hagin was very kind and cordial, putting to rest some of my nervousness. As the interview proceeded I was actually beginning to relax a little until Mrs. Hagin asked me that dreaded question, "Why do you want to work at RHEMA". Well I didn't know why, except that the Lord told me to go there and apply for a job. But I didn't want to tell her that because I figured she would think it a pretty shallow answer and that since it was Lord who said, she would think that I was trying to make her feel obligated to give me a job. Now I had owned my own business and was well acquainted with being on the other side of the table as an employer conducting an interview, and as the saying goes, "I have heard it all".

So as I am sitting there facing this question, a question I had hoped somehow would have miraculously disappeared, I am trying desperately to remember what I wrote on the application. After an unsuccessful attempt of trying to tap into my memory banks, I ended up giving her an answer that seemed to be acceptable. To this day I couldn't tell you if what I said agreed with what I wrote on the application. I left the interview on a high note and a couple of days later received a call informing me that I was to report to work the following day.

I did not really understand the significance of why the Lord wanted me to work there until several years later. I am so grateful for what RHEMA Bible Training Center has imparted to me. But I am also equally grateful for what was imparted to me during the two years I worked within the RHEMA organization. My job was not glamorous or financially lucrative, but I wouldn't change it for anything for it imparted to me things that I wouldn't have gotten anywhere else.

Many times the question people raise is "WHY". I do not ask this question of the Lord anymore because I have come to the understanding that God knows what He is doing better than I do. The Lord knows what is lacking and what is needed in fully equipping us to fulfill His call on our lives. Along the path of our pursuit of the call of God, He places us in strategic positions to teach us and impart to us those things that we are lacking and also to strengthen and undergird those things which we do have. He also puts us in these places to test our obedience, our attitudes and faithfulness. We may not know the why, see the importance, or understand the significance of it at the time. But as God promotes us step by step through our obedience and faithfulness, those seasons in our life become very precious to us.

Psalm 139:16
"You saw me before I was born. Every day of my life was recorded in your book. Every moment was laid out before a single day passed. How precious are your thoughts about me, O God! They are innumerable"!—(NLT)

Here in Psalm 139, the Bible declares that every moment of our lives has been written in the pages of God's book. This has often intrigued me and I am beginning to see that God's plan for our lives is like a book which contains many chapters, each chapter representing a season of time.

A book contains many chapters which progressively unveils the story inside. God's book concerning our individual lives also contains many chapters which progressively reveals God's will for us. There have been many chapters, or seasons of time in my life and attending RHEMA was one of those chapters or seasons of time.

As we faithfully fulfill each chapter or season of time, God opens to us the next chapter and moves us into our next season of time. Many times we want to hurry on to the next chapter but it is crucial that we remain patient and are faithful to finish the chapter we are in. In progressing through the chapters of God's book for our lives, we must complete each chapter before we can enter into the next. If we are going to run our race, finish and win the prize at the end, we must run according to the rules of the race. That means we cannot skip over any of the steps that God has laid before us.

In Colossians 4:17, Apostle Paul admonishes Archippus to take heed to the ministry which he received in the Lord, that he fulfill it. It would behoove us to take Paul's admonition to Archippus and apply it diligently to ourselves. We must take heed to the ministry that each of us have received in the Lord, that we fulfill it. Our ministry consists of whatever it is that God has us doing at the moment. We go from faith to faith, from glory to glory, but only as we obediently and faithfully take each step that the Lord places before us.

YOU HAVE TO LEAVE

We had been at RHEMA almost two years and now graduation was quickly approaching. The most commonly asked question around school was, "What are you going to do after graduation"?

I liked my job at RHEMA. I never thought that vacuuming carpets, scrubbing floors, washing windows, cleaning toilets, etc, etc. could be such a pleasure and blessing. I really enjoyed what I was doing and had fully intended on remaining there after graduation. However, just two weeks before graduation during worship on a Sunday morning, the Lord spoke to my heart and said, "You have to leave". I don't mean I heard an audible voice, although God does speak audibly from time to time, but the words came up out of my spirit like a still small voice. The Holy Spirit dwells in our spirit and God contacts us through our spirit. Proverbs 20:27 says that the spirit of man is the candle of the Lord. In other words, God will lead and guide us through our spirit. Well, I begin to cry and told the Lord I liked it at RHEMA and didn't want to leave. He said, "No, you have leave".

Coming from the interior of Alaska with its cold, snow and ice, I had come to appreciate the Oklahoma weather and although I loved Alaska, returning to a snow shovel was not all that appealing. I didn't realize it at the time, but moving back to Alaska was another chapter in my pursuit of the call of God and in this chapter were divine appointments that would propel us into our next phase of ministry.

In our pursuit of fulfilling God's plans and purposes for our lives, there will be those times when the Lord will say "you have to leave". God's chariot doesn't have a reverse, and if you are going to go with God, He will only take you forward. This of course, will at times necessitate leaving other things.

The call of God cannot be fulfilled by remaining where you are and at times involves abandoning things we have become secure and settled in. Pursuing the call of God is based upon faith in God and not in things that are comfortable or familiar to us.

After resigning my job at RHEMA, we stayed in Tulsa until the end of July and after Campmeeting loaded up our truck and embarked on our journey back to Alaska.

CHAPTER 9

You Are Going To Russia

After leaving RHEMA in the summer of 1993 and moving back to Alaska, rather than returning to Fairbanks where we had lived before going to Bible school, the Lord directed us to a small community about 45 miles north of Anchorage. There we got involved in a church doing what we could to be of help.

For some reason, God will give me direction or some form of instruction right in the middle of worship. On a Sunday morning in May of 1995 while I was absorbed in praise and worship, I heard these words, "you're going to Russia". Needless to say, I was no longer worshipping. It was so real to me that it jolted me right out of worship. It was like someone standing right next to me speaking but yet the words seem to come up out of my spirit, from inside me. I knew immediately that it was the Lord for I had heard Him speak to me on several other occasions and had come to know His voice.

Some people think it strange that you would hear God speak. But really we ought to think it strange that Christians do not hear and come to know the voice of God. Jesus talks about His sheep and points out the fact that His sheep "HEAR HIS VOICE" and they follow Him *(John 10:1-30)*.

Apostle Paul says in Romans 8:14 that the children of God are to be led by the Spirit of God. How does the Spirit of God lead us? Jesus gives us some insight into the leading of God in John 16:13-15; the Holy Spirit "SPEAKS" to us that which he hears from heaven. Well, I had become acquainted with the voice of God and knew it was God speaking. He said, "You're going to Russia".

My first thought was, what in the world am I going to go to Russia for? Other than praying for the nation of Russia, along with other nations of the world, I had no special place in my heart or burden for Russia. My only thoughts of Russia circled around ice, snow, cold etc. Not that I wasn't use to living in such conditions, after all, we lived over 14 years in the interior of Alaska where the winters were long, dark, and cold. But in thinking of Russia I always thought of it as being on the extreme side of unmitigated bleakness where people were sent as a form of punishment. I later learned that this wasn't exactly the case, although close, it wasn't exactly the case.

When inquiring why I went to Russia, people often ask if I had a special burden for Russia. My answer is always "NO". It wasn't a burden that inspired me to go to Russia; it was the will of God that impelled me. Of course after working fulltime in the Russian Far East for ten years I developed close relationships and a love for the Russian people. Prior to that, it was only the word of the Lord and my love for Him that motivated me to go. Now understand that the Lord can and does place a special burden, if you want to call it that, on people for certain nations or people groups. But with me, that was not the case. As I stated in the beginning of this book, there are many different ways in which God calls people to ministry. The method is not important. The important thing is that we heed the call and let God be God.

One mistake people commonly make is looking for the spectacular and as a result miss the supernatural. 1 Kings 19:9-16 gives us an example of the word of the Lord coming to Elijah concerning what God wanted him to do. The Bible says there was a great strong wind, but God wasn't in the wind. Then an earthquake, but God was not in the earthquake. After the earthquake there was a fire, but God was not in the fire. Then the Bible says there came to Elijah a still small voice and through the small still voice God spoke to Elijah telling him what he was to do.

Everything God does is supernatural, so we don't want ignore the still small voice. No matter what method God may use to call someone, it is a supernatural call. Don't seek God's will through seeking something spectacular. Let the word of the Lord come to you in the way God chooses.

SOME THINGS ARE BEST LEFT UNSAID

Galatians 1:15-16
But when it pleased God, who separated me from my mother's womb, and called me by his grace, to reveal his Son in me that I might preach him among the heathen; immediately I conferred not with flesh and blood.

There are some things that are best left unsaid, at least for a season. Apostle Paul, in referring to what God had revealed to him concerning his life, did not immediately go around sharing with everyone what God had revealed to him.

Some things God speaks to us about are sometimes, for a time at least, best left unsaid. What

I mean is that sometimes it is best not to say anything to anyone concerning what the Lord has said, or even share some experiences you may have had with the Lord. I am speaking here from my own experience. There were times when just out of excitement and enthusiasm, I have shared with others things God had revealed to me only to find those things being desecrated by sarcastic remarks coming through a cynical although sometimes well meaning Christian.

In Matthew 7:6, Jesus tells us not to give that which is holy to dogs, neither cast our pearls before swine. This is not a Bible lesson on dogs or swine but simply something that should be considered when it comes to sharing with others what God has revealed to us personally. The call of God is a precious thing and should be handled with great care and wisdom.

Neither dogs nor swine have any cognizance in recognizing or distinguishing what is precious and valuable and what is not. This reminds me of a dog we once had. I had bought a brand new pair of dress shoes and when I got home I took them out of the box and placed them alongside my other shoes. My wife and I went visiting that evening and when we returned home, there were my brand new shoes all chewed up. They were brand new; I hadn't even worn them yet!

It wouldn't have been so bad if the dog would have chewed up an old pair of shoes like my old worn out sneakers that were sitting right next to my brand new dress shoes. You see, the dog didn't know the difference, to him they were just something to chew on.

You could take a plain old worthless rock and a priceless diamond, place both of them in front of a pig and it wouldn't know the difference. To a pig they are the same and because of a lack of discernment, a lack of understanding. The pig's attitude toward and treatment of the priceless diamond would be no different than that of the plain old worthless rock. They would both be trampled into the mud and discarded.

Well, Jesus wasn't calling people dogs or swine and neither should we. Jesus was simply alluding to the fact that there are some things you shouldn't share with just anyone. In other words, we are to be careful with whom we share those things that are precious and valuable to us.

When God speaks to you in a very personal profound way, it is a very sacred and precious thing to you. Not everyone places the same value on them that you might. Jesus is saying that some people have no appreciation or comprehension of what has value and what doesn't. There are people who have no perception as to what is precious and what is not.

When it comes to the things of God many people, whether they realize it or not, behave like dogs or swine. There is no awareness or perception in regard to worth or value concerning things of a spiritual nature and as a result the things of God hold no place of significance where they are concerned. Many God given dreams and desires have been dashed to pieces and trampled into the mud by the skepticism and insensitivity of fellow Christians.

When the Lord spoke to me concerning going to Russia, like Paul, I didn't immediately confer with flesh and blood; in other words, another human being. I kept it to myself and conferred only with the Lord until the proper time. I didn't tell anyone what God had said about going to Russia, not even my wife. Let me make this very clear, I do not consider my wife to be like the dog or swine who has no understanding. My wife is very sensitive and takes the things of God seriously, especially those things that involve our lives or ministry. One reason I didn't say anything to her was because of my own feelings in the matter. Many times our feelings don't want to line up with what God says and it takes time to conform them to His will.

Like I said before, I had no special place in my heart for Russia and I was quite content right where I was. However, I didn't completely ignore what God said but talked to Him about it quite frequently in prayer.

About two months later, Joe Purcell, a missionary who had been working in the Russian Far East for several years, came to minister at the church we were attending. I didn't know at the time that he was also a RHEMA graduate and that his ministry was based in Alaska. When Joe found out that we had also attended REHMA he approached my wife about the possibility of her helping with their state-side ministry affairs while they were abroad. My wife of course accepted, worked for them for the next three years and through this relationship we became good friends.

Now I had not said anything to my wife or to Joe what God had said to me about going to Russia. This of course would have been a perfect opportunity to try to open a door to Russia. After all, God did tell me I was going to Russia, and now we were involved with missionaries who are working in Russia. Why not just drop a few hints here and there and try to get them to invite me to Russia?

As reasonable as it may seem, it is not God's way of doing things. God says in His Word that a man's gift makes room for him and brings him before great men. I figured if I go to Russia it will have to be God and not me. Besides, I didn't have a great love affair for Russia and if God wanted me to go to it would have to be Him opening the door and making the way. So I said nothing, not even a hint about my call to Russia, neither to my wife or to Joe. This didn't mean I sat by and did nothing. I stayed hooked up in the church, helped wherever I could and eventually the pastor began having me teach every Wednesday night.

Three years had now passed since God told me I was going to Russia. I am teaching regularly on Wednesday nights, preaching occasionally on Sundays and doing what I knew to do. On one of these Wednesday nights that I was teaching, Joe and his wife Mary happened to be in attendance. After the service was over I was approached by Joe and asked to pray about joining them on the mission field in Russia. I knew right away in my heart that this was what God wanted us to do but told him we would pray about it, which we did. A few days later we met with Joe and Mary and told them we would join them. It was at that time I shared with them what the Lord had told me three years earlier. It was also at this time my wife heard it for the first time.

I didn't have to pray for my wife's preparation like I did when we went to Bible school because God had already been preparing her heart for the mission field through her working for Joe and Mary as their stateside secretary.

Marlene testified to this when Joe asked her how she felt about going to Russia. She said she knew in her heart that God was preparing her for something even though she didn't know exactly what it was. When it came time to step into what God had for us, there was no hesitation and there was no disagreement because we both had the witness in our hearts that this was the will of God.

This was one of the divine appointments God had arranged several years before when he told me we had to leave RHEMA and return to Alaska.

THE TIME FACTOR

I believe many times in our sincere desire and fervor to serve God and fulfill His will for our lives, we get ahead of God. People often try to force doors open by trying to influence their way into ministry and thereby getting themselves into difficulty which often leads to disillusionment and discouragement. This brings to light a deadly factor that I found I had to deal with in my own life and minister. It is what I call the "Time Factor".

Time seems to have a way of dissolving away all hope and expectation which often and brings you to the place of even questioning and doubting whether you heard from God or not. I am convinced this is one of the things Abraham had to deal with regarding God's promise to him concerning having a son by his wife Sarah, which of course was Isaac.

When the Lord told me to leave RHEMA, He didn't tell me why I had to leave, He didn't tell me the purposes behind having to leave. After moving back to Alaska we settled in the city of Wasilla. I took a job in Anchorage and begin making the daily 45 mile trip back and forth to work.

After nearly two years had passed I started getting a little antsy and begin questioning the Lord about why we came back to Alaska. I told Him there was nothing I was doing in Alaska that I couldn't have done at RHEMA. It wasn't long after this conversation that He told me I was going to Russia. Well, this didn't bring a lot of comfort to my flesh, but I did hear from God, I did receive a word from Him.

I continued with my job in Anchorage and another two years had passed since the Lord told me I was going to Russia. I had a very good job with excellent benefits and I was making top wages. Naturally speaking it couldn't be any better. But in my spirit I was becoming restless and not happy with what I was doing.

I would always try to get to work a couple of hours before anyone else each morning and spend time praying before starting the day's work. One morning I was especially discouraged and felt that I would forever be trapped in this seemingly going nowhere situation. I seemed to be losing sight of what God had placed in my heart. I knew I was losing it, I could sense it and it concerned me. I was thinking maybe I didn't really hear God, or maybe God had changed His mind. All of these things were bombarding my mind and it seemed as if all hope, and certainly my expectations were fading away.

As I was praying that morning with all of this on my mind and pouring my heart out to God, I asked the Lord, "How much longer?" Then came that still small voice saying, "Soon, just a little bit longer"! Well, this brought some reassurance and comfort to my heart but another year passed by before that "Soon, just a little bit longer" materialized.

I share this because there is some truth here. The "Time Factor" can be deadly to the call of God on a person's life. The "Time Factor" is simply the duration of time between receiving a word from the Lord and the manifestation of that word. Time will put pressure on your faith and if you are not careful, it will break you down to a level of discouragement where you begin believing and speaking the wrong things. Time will try to pull you away from the word of the Lord that has come to you and bring you to the place where you give up on it and take another path. The "Time Factor" can also cause people to do things to try to pry open doors; to try to help God out so to speak.

> *Hebrews 10:35-36*
> *Do not cast away your confidence (faith) which has great reward. For you have need of endurance (patience) so that after you have done the will of God (willingly obeyed) you may receive the promise (the manifestation of the word of the Lord).*

If you know that you know that you know you have a word from God, don't allow the "Time Factor" to pressure you into giving up or doing something you shouldn't to try to help God out. Time can be a friend or a foe, depending on how you look at and treat time.

Regardless of time, we should always remember that God is faithful. We should always endeavor to remember that God is for us and that He will make good His word concerning our lives. All He needs from us is willing obedience, steadfast faith, and patience.

CHAPTER 10

The Power of Grace

2 Corinthians 12:9

My grace is sufficient for thee: for my strength is made perfect in weakness.

In the next two chapters, we will look at two essential elements involved with pursuing the call of God. One is the grace of God that is sufficient for all things and the other is the peace of God which surpasses all understanding. I call these the "Essential Duo" because they are inseparable twins. By this I mean where there is grace there is peace and where there is peace there is grace.

There are many things that are rarely spoken of concerning fulfilling the call of God and we often may find ourselves wondering if there is anyone else experiencing the same things we are.

As missionaries home from the field, we talk of the great things that God has done and is doing. We talk of what a great year it was, and truly it was. But we seldom, if ever, speak about the things that take place behind the scenes so to speak. We don't discuss times of hardship, times of heartache or distress. We don't speak of the times of utter despair and discouragement. We don't speak of the times of weeping and crying out before God. We don't talk of times when our hearts become so overwhelmed that it feels as though they will burst if there is no release. It is in times like these that we need something much greater and higher than ourselves.

I am not implying that ministry is hard and burdensome, quite the contrary. Ministry that is done within the will of God is easy, light, joyous and rewarding even in the midst of trials and adversity. But what I am saying is this; ministers are human just like everyone else and as such must deal with the human factor which tends to want to step out of line when facing obstacles and adversity in life or ministry. Just because a person is right in the center of God's perfect will does not mean you are exempt from adversity or the feelings and emotions that the pressures of everyday life and ministry can bring.

In Psalm 61:1-3 we see David, who faced such times, crying out to God, *"Hear my cry, O God; attend unto my prayer. From the end of the earth will I cry unto thee, when my heart is overwhelmed: lead me to the rock that is higher than I".* David goes on to say in verse 3, *"For thou hast been a shelter for me and a strong tower from the enemy".*

I believe with all my heart that what David found in the shelter and strong tower of God was the all sufficient grace of God. Hebrews 4:16 tells us to *"come boldly to the throne of grace",* I like that. God's throne is a throne of grace! The writer goes on to say, "That we may obtain mercy and *find grace* in time of need."

Throughout his writings, Paul an Apostle of God, a preacher and teacher of the Gospel of Christ, speaks of being troubled on every side; being persecuted, cast down, being beaten, encountering perils of all sorts, having fears within and fears without. In the midst of his crying out to God, in 2 Corinthians 12:9 we see God leading him to the shelter and high tower of His all sufficient grace.

Following the call of God on your life is not always a road of ease. Just because you are in the perfect will of God doesn't mean you won't face adversity. I have come to realize, and I believe Scripture substantiates this, that the call of God cannot be fulfilled without learning the lessons of God's grace.

GOD'S GRACE TEACHES US

1 Peter 4:10 speaks of the manifold grace of God. This simply means that there are many facets to the grace of God. The grace of God is often taught from a doctrinal standpoint and there are probably as many definitions of grace as there are facets of grace.

Much of my understanding of grace came from what I learned from teachings I had received in church, Sunday school, Bible school, books, and other forms of media. However, it has become clear to me that gaining an unfeigned understanding of grace is like gaining an unquestionable understanding of God. I can learn and know some things about God on a doctrinal or intellectual level, and that's good, but to really know what is in the heart and mind of God I must personally experience God on an intimate level. This is true of any relationship. I can know some things about a person, but just knowing some things about them is not the same as truly knowing them. The closer I get to someone through fellowship the more I come to know and understand who that person really is and what they are all about. The same is true concerning the grace of God.

Most Christians could probably give a doctrinally correct explanation of grace from what they have learned from various forms of media. But what about a genuine explanation of the grace of God from what grace itself has taught them?

We can learn and know some things about grace on a doctrinal or intellectual level, which is good, but to fully understand grace one must go beyond merely a doctrinal or intellectual knowledge of God's grace; we must fellowship with His grace.

Titus 3:11-12 reveals something that the grace of God does—GRACE TEACHES US. There is what we could call the School of Grace, and the lessons to be taught can only be learned within the confines of grace. In other words, if I am going to really understand grace beyond just an intellectual level, I am going to have to be in the place where the grace of God is actively operating in my life. I must allow grace to teach me about grace, and that can only be done through intimate encounters with the grace of God. Veritable understanding of God's grace comes the same way a genuine understanding of God Himself comes; "Through Intimacy".

God's grace is sufficient for all things, which means Grace is that which goes beyond our own abilities, beyond our capacity to persevere. It is that which goes beyond our own power or strength enabling us to take on and execute any God given task. Grace is a divine empowerment that will carry you over in times of adversity and weakness, in times when your heart is overwhelmed.

It is grace that teaches us about the faithfulness of God. It is grace that reveals the depths of His love for us. It is grace that teaches us to stand fast in the faith. It is grace that teaches us to trust and obey, to be totally dependent on God and no one else. It is grace that teaches us to be strong and of good courage. It is grace that teaches us about the peace of God that surpasses all understanding.

The Bible says that the steps of a righteous man are ordered of God. I have found that progressing to the next step, even though it is ordered by God, is not always pleasant even if it is a promotion. It is only by the grace of God that I am able to move forward and walk in what has been ordered. It wasn't until I had entered fulltime ministry as a missionary that I really began to learn what the grace and peace of God was all about. God is always there to help us, but many times we frustrate His grace by neglecting to use some of the tools He has given us, such as prayer and faith, which allows His grace to work on our behalf.

In Galatians 2:21 Paul says, *"I do not frustrate the grace of God . . ."* The word frustrate means to cast off or to set aside as having no value. It means to despise, reject, to nullify or make void, or to neutralize. When God said my grace is sufficient for you, He revealed that His grace is a spiritual law or spiritual force. To frustrate the grace of God carries the idea of depriving the law of grace its power by embracing opinions or acts that are opposed to it.

As I look back on my life, I see where there were times when I frustrated the grace of God through disobedience, unbelief, and through just simply being unwilling to be in an uncomfortable place. Anytime I draw back from God's way, I frustrate the grace of God and never learn what grace had to teach me, which I might add, I will have to learn later. The grace of God can't teach me its lessons through books and study, but only through direct intimate contact with grace itself. God's grace is sufficient for all things regardless of the task ahead or the circumstance or situation, but I must allow it to work in the midst of my circumstance or situation.

In referring to the grace of God, Paul says in Romans 5:2 that it takes faith to gain access into that grace. Faith requires fortitude, stamina and tenacity.

It requires a complete abandonment of fear, doubt and self-sufficiency, placing total dependency on God alone.

Our first few years in Russia were spent in the city of Khabarovsk after which we relocated our base of operation to the city of Ussuriisk. After several years in the city of Ussuriisk, I begin to sense a stirring in my heart concerning a change coming our way. It was just a knowing on the inside of me just like I had when the Lord moved us from Khabarovsk. The only difference in this situation was instead of ignoring the stirring in my heart, I immediately went into prayer about it.

Several days later as I was walking from my office to the kitchen to get a drink of water, I suddenly stopped dead in my tracks. Something dropped into my spirit. I felt the weight of it just as you would feel the weight of something heavy being dropped into a bag you were holding. Sometimes it is hard to explain spiritual things, and I can't explain how I knew, but I knew exactly what it was that dropped into my spirit. I suddenly knew I was going to be pastoring and the grace to pastor had just dropped into my spirit.

Although at that particular time I didn't know where or when I would be pastoring, I kept it immersed in prayer. About a year later the Lord revealed to me exactly what church I would be pastoring and that I would be there three years. I kept all this to myself and another year passed before I was approached about taking that very church.

We took a church that was suffering from severe internal problems and was on the verge of disintegration. Had I known everything there was to know about the church, I may have had second thoughts and needed some extra prodding about taking it. I believe this is one reason why God doesn't reveal everything to us.

Even though the Lord had given me step by step instructions concerning the church, the first year seemed to be nothing but frustration after frustration. There were many times I wanted to sneak out to the airport and catch the first plane out of there without telling anyone we were leaving. But I also knew that pastoring this church was the will of God and it was only by the grace of God that we were able to stay hooked up and faithful to what God wanted to accomplish there. I asked the Lord once why he sent us to pastor this church. He said, "Two reasons; First, I have given you what these people need and secondly, I want to teach you about people".

NEVER UNDERESTIMATE
THE POWER OF GRACE

God does not ask us to do the things that are naturally easy for us. He only asks us to do the things that we are perfectly fit to do through His grace. We never want to underestimate the power of God's grace. No matter what God may ask us to do, we are perfectly fit and perfectly equipped to accomplish the things He asks. God will never ask us to go anywhere or do anything without His grace to sustain us. It is only by the grace of God through faith that I am able to patiently run the race that is set before me. There is much that can be said about the grace of God, but here I can only allude to it as God's divine influence upon one's life both to will and to do of His good pleasure.

I have experienced times of despair, times of adversity, and I thank God for his all sufficient grace by which He will always leads me in triumphant victory.

On a foreign mission field, especially when you are alone, by that I mean there are no people of your own race, culture, or language with which to fellowship, many times there is a sense of isolation and aloneness in endeavoring to carry out your God given assignments. I have my wife who is with me every day but I am very careful about voicing my disappointments, frustrations and despair with her. These kinds of things can be contagious and it is very easy for even those around you to catch your consternation causing further dismay.

It is what grace has taught us over the years that sustain us through challenges and adversities that try to break us down by probing for weaknesses in the bulwark of our faith.

HOW'S NINEVEH?

On one of our state-side visits, a close friend of mine asked me in a joking sort of way, "How's Nineveh"? Well I knew exactly what he meant and chuckled at his question. He had been to the Russian Far East and was familiar with the conditions in that part of the world. To Jonah, Nineveh was far from an ideal place for ministry but yet God told him to go there.

We may have a "Nineveh" that God sends us to but it's important to learn the lessons involved with whatever our "Nineveh" may representative of in our pursuit of God's objectives for our lives.

Jonah considered Nineveh a less than desirable place and expected God to see it in the same light.

Jonah was so engrossed and preoccupied with his own discomfort that he failed to learn what God was trying to teach him.

The real lesson that God was trying to get over to Jonah was that His grace wasn't just for the easy and pleasurable places but also for the less desirable places such as Nineveh. God sent Jonah to Nineveh as a vessel of His grace so that through Jonah God could reveal and extend His grace to the people of Nineveh.

Maybe you are in a "Nineveh", a less than desirable place. But it is important to understand that God chooses people to send to places such as "Nineveh" for one purpose; so that the same grace that He has shown us can be made known to those He sends us to. The Bible says Jesus came full of grace to a corrupt and sinful world. As ambassadors of Christ, no less is expected of us.

Without the grace of God we would not be able to do what we are doing. I believe the grace of God is a supernatural impartation to stand and not give up. I am convinced that it is the power of this grace that has further captured and bound me to the holy calling of God.

Apostle Paul says it is by the grace of God that we are what we are and it is by faith that we stand in this grace. The grace of God has some marvelous things to teach, but it requires obedience, faith, and humility on our part.

Putting the old hymn Amazing Grace into modern words; it is grace that has brought me safely this far and it is grace that will continually lead me on until I cross the finish line. Thank God for His amazing grace!

CHAPTER 11

Incomprehensible Peace

Philippians 4:6-7

Be careful for nothing, but in everything by prayer and supplication with thanksgiving let your requests be known unto God. And the peace of God, which passeth all understanding, shall keep your hearts and minds through Christ Jesus.

The other member of this essential duo in fulfilling divine assignments is the PEACE OF GOD. There is a difference between peace "WITH" God and the peace "OF" God. Peace "WITH" God comes through Jesus Christ and the new birth. But the peace "OF" God is an inner tranquility which is imparted to keep our heart and mind in perfect peace in the midst of life's storms and every kind of test, trial or circumstance.

It never ceases to amaze me, when in the midst of trouble and adversity, how serene one can be. During my first year on the mission field I was invited to conduct a seminar in the city of Aldan located in central Siberia. I of course was excited about the prospect and my Russian brother Grecia, whom I had come to love and respect very much, would accompany me.

Just a couple days before we were to leave I got a phone call from Grecia with some disturbing news. In the process of preparing for the trip to Aldan I was told not to be concerned about bringing an interpreter because one would be provided.

But now Grecia calls and says, "Gary, I just found out today that the interpreter is not a Christian, they are hoping she will get saved while interpreting for you". Well, I could appreciate what they were thinking, however, I had an undeniable check in my spirit. This was not just preach a Sunday sermon and go home. This trip entailed three meetings a day for six days and it was far too late to make arrangements for another interpreter.

I was working under Joe Purcell and I quickly made a phone call to Joe for some much needed advice. As I told him about the interpreter there was what seemed to me a long period of silence. Then I heard Joe say, "Well, I have done it, it can be done" and he encouraged me to proceed with the trip. I had also received other pieces of disturbing news that could be cause for concern but the Word of God tells us to be anxious for nothing, but in everything with prayer and supplication with thanksgiving, let our requests be made known to God; and the peace of God which passes all understanding will guard our hearts and minds through Christ Jesus. As I prayed, I asked the Lord specifically if I should go or not go due to the current situation. The Lord spoke very clearly saying "GO" so I went.

We boarded the train in Khabarovsk embarking on a thirty eight and a half hour trip to the city of Neryungri where we were to be picked up by motor vehicle and transported to Aldan. It was very early morning when we arrived in Neryungri and upon disembarking from the train we were greeted by the chilling forty seven below zero Siberian winter.

I was no stranger by any means to this kind of cold having lived many years in the interior of Alaska where temperatures of this sort were common and often remained for days and even weeks at a time. However, I had taken an American brother with me who had come on a short term mission assignment. He was from the southern part of the United States and the sub-zero temperatures were not befriending him at all.

Discovering our transportation to Aldan had not arrived yet, we went inside the train depot to escape the bitter cold but found it wasn't much warmer inside. After a couple hours our ride finally arrived and we were off on the four and a half hour drive to Aldan.

THE PEACE THAT SURPASSES
ALL UNDERSTANDING

You don't have to be in a foreign country very long before you realize you are not in the United States of America where we take for granted even the simplest freedom we enjoy such as driving. The Russian road system is strewn not only with potholes large enough to swallow a car whole, but also with law enforcement check points complete with personnel armed with automatic weapons.

We passed through a small village called Chulman and several miles down the road came to one of these check points and of course we were stopped. The authorities commenced to pull all documents for the vehicle and also the passports of everyone in the van. It wasn't until sometime later that I learned why they had taken all passports, which they normally don't do with the exception of the driver. There are certain cities classified as "closed cities" and special documents are required to enter them. Aldan was one of these cities and so everyone's documents were examined.

After several minutes of sitting in the van, I could sense my Russian brothers becoming somewhat uneasy and were in deep conversation with one another. They then left the van and went into the guard-shack leaving me and my American brother sitting in the van. After about 45 minutes I began to wonder what was going on. Just then a militia car pulled up to the small guard-shack and two militia-men went inside.

Another 30 minutes passes by, and by this time all the windows on the van were frosted over and we could no longer see out. All of a sudden the van door slid open and there stood two militia-men one of whom in a booming voice said, "You and you out"!— pointing his finger at me and my American brother. They took us into custody, put us in the militia car and roared away leaving all our Russian brothers behind. I took a peek out the rear window as we were being scurried away and saw them all running to the van. It comforted me to know that they hadn't abandoned us but were following along behind. We were taken back to the village of Chulman, escorted into the militia station and put in a small room under guard.

Although there may be times of doubts and fears as to where God is leading, I have learned that God will never lead you where His grace cannot sustain you. The grace and peace of God is a place of rest in God, a place where you lay aside dependency upon your own efforts, abilities and reasoning, and embark on trusting that God knows what He is doing. God's grace is the place where we are taken beyond our natural selves and divinely empowered and enabled for whatever lies ahead of us.

Almost two hours had passed by and we are still sitting in this room with a guard at the door. In the distance I could faintly hear what sounded like very intense arguing taking place. Little did I know that it was over the question of, "What are these Americans doing here"?

After nearly two hours, we were retrieved by the guard outside the door and taken down a long dark hallway to another room. As we approached I spotted Grecia standing up against the wall and the undeniable expression on his face clearly revealed that this was a very serious matter and things were not exactly in a harmonious state.

We were escorted through a series of rooms and the discussion which I faintly heard earlier was now coming through loud and clear. We were taken into the room from which all the commotion was coming and quickly discovered it was the Commanders office.

After we took a seat I just sat there listening to the conversation between the commander and the associate pastor from Aldan who was sent to pick us up. I knew very little Russian at that time and didn't understand what was being said, however, it didn't take a rocket scientist to figure out that there was yet no resolve to our presence.

As I sat there listening, I felt rather strange because in spite of what was happening I had this inner peace that I couldn't explain or understand. I felt utterly detached from the situation and this seemingly unnatural phlegmatic feeling left me thinking there must be something wrong with me.

In light of our predicament, I had no sense of fear, anxiety or concern. I searched for it and even told myself, "Gary, this is weird, it's not normal, you should be doing something! Shouldn't you be at least a little bit worried"? I look over at my American brother and could clearly see he was not experiencing what I was experiencing. He was white as a sheet and notably worried. Though things were in turmoil around me,

I had a perfect inner peace that my natural human reasoning couldn't comprehend.

As the conversation continued, I reminded the Lord that I had asked whether or not I should go and that He had said "GO". I told Him since it was He who told me to go, and I was simply obeying what He said to do, this problem was not mine but His and it needed to be fixed. I then began to pray silently in other tongues.

After several minutes of praying silently in other tongues, all of a sudden, just like someone would turn off a light switch, the room became absolutely silent. No one said a word, no one moved; everyone just sat there staring blankly straight ahead.

After what seemed like an eternity to me of unbroken silence, the commander pulled out a piece of paper, laid it on the desk, looked at the associate pastor from Aldan and said, "Make out an invitation for Gary and his friend". After the invitation was made out for us, the commander signed it, put his official stamp on it, handed back all our documents and we were off to Aldan.

As we drove back toward Aldan, buzzing on through the check point where we were stopped, the Lord brought to my remembrance the scripture that says, "When a man's ways please the Lord, He makes even his enemies to be at peace with him". Praise the Lord!

When you have been captured by the Holy Calling of God, no matter what the circumstance may be, there is a supernatural peace that will come into your heart and mind that surpasses all understanding bringing perfect rest. Just like the account of Peter's arrest in Acts chapter twelve. He had been arrested, put in prison, even chained between two guards just to make sure he didn't escape because the next day King Herod was planning to make an open spectacle of Peter by putting him to death.

As we read the account, instead of seeing a perturbed Peter biting his finger nails, sitting up all night worrying over his dilemma and what was going to happen to him, we see him fast asleep chained between two prison guards. Perfect sleep in those kinds of situations can only come when there is perfect peace. Peter was so fast asleep that the Bible says when the Angel came to rescue Peter he had to actually give Peter a good hard jab in the side in order to wake him up. Now that's peaceful sleeping.

I believe God allows us to experience certain things not only for the exercising and testing of our faith, but to teach us how to recognize and be led or governed by his peace.

Many decisions are made based upon the physical senses and natural human reasoning. These things have their place, but when whole heartedly following after God and you know that you are doing what you are suppose to be doing, you must learn to be governed or ruled by the peace of God.

I have been in many situations since in which I knew I was in the place I was supposed to be, doing what I was supposed to be doing, and everything I was seeing, hearing, and feeling through my natural senses would propagate fear striving to get me to think and act contrary. But when I knew I was in God's plan, regardless of what was going on around on the outside, I had perfect peace on the inside.

You cannot judge whether or not you are in the perfect will of God by how well or how bad things are going or by looking at the outward appearance of situations. You can only judge by the peace of what you know God has revealed on the inside of you.

God will often put you in positions outside your comfort zone and above your own natural abilities. In these places, your physical senses and own human reasoning will always engender fear and doubt.

The peace of God is something you look for on the inside of you, not in what is occurring around you. If there is no inner peace or rest, then it's time to step back and evaluate the situation.

Jesus said in John 15:5 that without him we can do nothing. The call of God always places you above what you yourself are capable of and it is the all sufficient grace of God and the peace that surpasses all understanding that helps gets you there.

I was once asked by a Russian pastor, "Aren't you afraid to be here?" I replied "No". He gave me a bit of a startled look and I proceeded to tell Him about the grace and the peace of God that comes with doing what God called you to do. Don't think he ever heard that before.

When you have been captured by the Holy Calling of God, like Apostle Paul, you will go bound in the spirit even when you know there is trouble waiting ahead *(Acts 20:22)*. God never promised we wouldn't face difficulty, adversity or danger. But He did promise to never leave us or forsake us. He did promise that no matter what we are facing, He will lead us in triumphant victory. He promised that even though we may be walking through the shadow of the valley of death we do not have to fear for He is with us and for us. I don't know about you but that alone brings peace to me.

When we made the move from Russia to Thailand the Lord did not speak to me like He did when he sent me to Russia. What then helped me make the decision? I followed the peace I had on the inside concerning the move. I had the witness of the Holy Spirit on the inside of me that this was the right thing to do. In other words, it seemed good to me and the Holy Spirit.

We can be led by the peace of God on the inside of us just as we can be led by hearing God's voice. This is something that is learned as you walk with God. Many times the leading of the peace of God is missed because we are seeking a voice.

In Colossians 3:15 Apostle Paul's exhortation is for us to let the peace of God rule in our hearts. This simply means to follow the leading of the peace of God on the inside of you. many times in regard to the leading of the Holy Spirit, the leading will be simply manifested through a sense of peace in your heart. This peace is the "witness" of the Holy Spirit that it is the proper thing.

THE ESENTIAL DUO

The Grace of God and the Peace of God

Do not forsake or frustrate the grace that is yours through Christ Jesus. Stand strong in the grace that is in Christ Jesus and let the peace of God rule in your heart.

CHAPTER 12

A Place of God's Choosing

Genesis 12:1-2

Now the Lord had said to Abram: "Get out of your country, from your family and from your father's house, to a land that I will show you [2] I will make you a great nation; I will bless you and make your name great; and you shall be a blessing."

In this chapter I will try to shine some light on questions I believe most everyone who has committed to the call of God has faced in some form or another. Questions such as; why do you go to the foreign mission field, why do you have to serve God in such a far off place, why can't you stay home and serve God? Sometimes, even those people God is calling ask God the same questions.

First of all, we must address the issue of what is "home" for a servant of God. For someone who is pursuing the plans and purposes of God for their life, "home" is always the place of God's choosing. Within verses 1 and 2 of Genesis chapter 12 we can gain an understanding of exactly what the call of requires and its concomitant factors.

It all started for Abraham when the Lord said to him, "Get out of your country, from your family, and from your father's house, to a land that I will show you." In essence, God told Abraham to leave where he was and "GO" to another "PLACE". God was asking Abraham to leave the things he knew and was acquainted with; leave the things that were familiar and comfortable to him. Abraham was being asked to leave behind old relationships, family ties and people he loved. The first thing revealed here in the call of Abraham is that the call of God involves a place of God's choosing.

Everyone has a call on their life and that call, just as we see concerning the call of Abraham, involves a place of God's choosing. We go to the foreign field and serve God in far way places because it is the place of God's choosing where our life is concerned. It is not a place that I choose for myself but that God himself chooses for me. We cannot separate being in the will of God from being in the place of God's choosing because they are traveling companions.

THERE IS A PLACE OF GOD'S CHOOSING

There is a place of God's choosing. It is a place of blessing and increase. It is a place where you will grow and develop like never before. It is a place of divine appointments and associations. It is a place of great grace and anointing, a place where you will experience fulfillment and satisfaction. It is a wealthy place where you will flourish and become everything God intends. It is a place where the value of your gifts and graces will be developed and released causing you to become a great blessing to the Body of Christ and the world around you.

Genesis 12:2-3 reveals seven promises that God made to Abraham concerning the place of God's choosing for him.

1. I will make you a great nation.

2. I will bless you.

3. I will make you great.

4. You shall be a blessing.

5. I will bless those who bless you.

6. I will curse those who curse you.

7. In you shall all the families of the earth be blessed.

All of these promises were contingent upon Abraham "GOING" to the place of God's choosing. In order for Abraham to receive the blessings of the promises, he had to "GO" where God told him to go. In other words, he would not have been blessed by staying where he was when God told him to go to another place.

God has destined all of us for blessing and greatness but this blessing and greatness is only found in the place of God's choosing. There are some who would probably argue this point, but if you study the lives of all the great men and women of God, you will find that they were blessed and became great because they obeyed and went to the place of God's choosing. There have been people who have tried to convince me that staying in my own country of the United States was the safest and most provisional place to be. But what they fail to understand is that the safest and most blessed provisional place for me, or any other Christian, is in the place of God's choosing. If God called me to serve Him in my own country, I would gladly obey and serve Him faithfully.

The place of God's choosing is not just a place geographically speaking, but also a place spiritually. The call of God has periodically moved us from one place to another and in the early years of ministry I viewed these moves only from a natural geographical point of view. In other words, I only thought of it as just relocating to some other place on the planet. But as I looked back at where we had been and where we presently were, I realized that the places of God's choosing were not just geographical places on the planet earth, but that every place naturally speaking is also a place spiritually speaking.

What I mean is this. Every time we have gone to the place of God's choosing, the challenges we faced in those places caused spiritual growth and development in our personal lives as well as our ministry. With each place of God's choosing we were brought to a higher level of faith and spiritual maturity. People are often deceived by thinking that these levels of increase will come no matter where they are or what they are doing. These levels of increase cannot be attained anywhere except in the place of God's choosing.

When God told me to go to RHEMA Bible Training Center it meant leaving the security of our jobs. It meant leaving our home, our possessions and our friends. It meant leaving where we were and going to a place we had never been before, a place we knew nothing about. But when we went, there in the place of God's choosing we were blessed, there we grew and developed, there God begin to mold and shape us into the vessels He desired. It was there in the place of God's choosing that He brought into our lives divine associations and relationships that are still impacting and blessing us today. This would never have been unless we had obeyed God and went to the place of His choosing. Never despise or question the place of God's choosing for you because it is your place of blessing and greatness.

Upon graduating RHEMA Bible Training Center, the Lord said we were to go back to Alaska which meant leaving things behind again. Upon returning to Alaska, the Lord sent us not to Fairbanks where we had previously lived but to a place we were not familiar with. But in that place, we again encountered divine appointments and associations orchestrated by God that we would have missed had we not gone back to Alaska to the place of His choosing. It was in that place that the gifts, the grace, and the anointing that God placed upon my life begin to really develop.

When God called us into fulltime ministry as missionaries to a foreign field, again it involved leaving what we had become comfortable and familiar with. It meant leaving loved ones we knew we would not see for extended periods of time and going to the place of God's choosing.

At times it may seem that God is leading you to a place that is less than desirable. But the place of God's choosing is not something worse, it is something better, it is something of greater blessing.

TEMPORAL AND ETERNAL
REWARD AND BLESSING

It is important to understand that these places of God's choosing carry temporal rewards and blessing as well as great eternal rewards and blessing. Temporal rewards and blessing during our present life here on earth. Eternal rewards and blessing after this present life as we know it is over and we have stepped over into glory.

When considering the call of God we must look beyond our temporal life in this present world and look at eternity. If you are in a place and God has not told you to move from that place, then stay put because it is your place of reward and blessing not only for this present world, but also for the world to come.

The place God has for you does not necessarily mean you are supposed to be a missionary, or in any other type of fulltime ministry. Even if you are not called to fulltime ministry, God still has a place of His choosing for you.

Everyone born again believer has a God appointed place in the body of Christ *(1 Corinthians 12:18)*. God has a specific local church where he wants you to get hooked up and involved. It is a place where the Potter forms the clay into the vessel of His choosing. It is a place where we are fruitful, a place where the blessing of God empowers us and enables us to flourish in that place of God's choosing.

Abraham had to be in the place of God's choosing before he could experience the promises made to him. We also must be in the place of God's choosing before we can reap the benefits and blessings that following the call of God will bring into our lives and ministries.

The question that must be answered is; are we listening for and responding to our call? You may not know everything pertaining to your call; you may not see the whole picture yet. But our walk is not a walk of the natural senses but a walk of faith.

In speaking of Abraham, Hebrews 11:8 says, *"By faith Abraham, when he was called to go out into a place which he would receive as an inheritance, obeyed; and he went out, not knowing where he was going."* God simply said to Abraham "leave" and Abraham obeyed not knowing all the details.

Sometimes people make going to the place of God's choosing difficult by asking questions like, "Why must I leave?" They make statements like, "I need some security; I can't just leave everything and go; I need a place to live; I need a job; I need money; what about this and what about that." Understand that once we have heard from the Lord, all those questions and worries are insignificant. God is not ignorant of the things we have need of. If God has said GO, it means He has already got it all figured out.

In scripture, God reveals Himself as "Jehovah Jireh" which means the Lord who see's and makes provision *(Exodus 22:14).* He knows exactly what we are going to need and makes provision for every aspect of our going and dwelling in the place of His choosing. This doesn't mean that we throw common sense and wisdom out the window. Along with the word "GO" God gives us practical steps and things to do through which He helps make provision. We cannot just throw everything to the wind and move forward on presumption. Presumption is not faith.

We don't have to know all the details in order to walk by faith. The problem is that our human nature, that is our flesh, wants all the answers. We want God to sit down and describe every detail so we know what we are going to do and what is going to happen before we will get up and obey God. Many do not go to the place of God's choosing because they do not know what they will encounter along the way. God gives us what we need to know for the moment and what He does give us is always sufficient until He gives us more. Our responsibility is not to question the place of God's choosing but to simply obey and GO.

In 1 Kings Chapter 17, the Bible gives us some examples of God's provisional blessings in the places of His choosing. The prophet Elijah had proclaimed a drought upon the land and in verses 3-4 the Lord speaks to Elijah telling him to get away from where he was and go to the Brook Cherith which was a place of God's choosing.

What God said to Elijah next is important for us to see. God said to Elijah, I have commanded the ravens to feed you "THERE" *(vs. 4)*. Then in verse 8-9 we see the Lord telling Elijah to "GO" to a place called Zarephath for "THERE" He had commanded a widow to provide for him. These are only two of many examples of God's provisional blessings that we find throughout the Bible.

Not only is the place of God's choosing a place of supernatural provision, but it is also a place where great miracles can be wrought in our lives. In the Bible it is revealed that even miracles can be contingent upon obeying God and going to the place of His choosing.

Example: The leper Naaman was told to go not to just any river, but the river Jordan, and "THERE" he received his healing miracle *(2 Kings 5:1-14)*. The blind man was told to go and wash in the pool Siloam and "THERE" he received his miracle of sight *(John 9:1-7)*.

Throughout the Bible we see the command to "GO," but going to the place of God's choosing does not mean it will be easy. The Bible calls the devil our adversary and his only goal is to steal, kill, and destroy. The devil wants to keep you in a desolate place where you have no aspirations or vision. The devil will use people, circumstances, and even your own flesh to try to convince you not to go to the place of God's choosing. But when you make the commitment and by faith go to the place of God's choosing for you, the blessing of His promises comes on you and you flourish. Ephesians 3:20 says that God is able to do exceedingly, abundantly above all that we ask or think. God has a vision for you, a vision of increase, a vision of greatness, a vision of fruitfulness and influence in this world that far exceeds anything you can even imagine.

Let's look at something else God said to Abraham that we should take to heart and remember. After Abraham had entered into the place of God's choosing the Lord told Abraham, *"Do not be afraid Abraham I am your shield, your exceedingly great reward"* *(Genesis 15:1).*

We do not need be fearful of going to and dwelling in the place of God's choosing. God is still the same God he was when He spoke to Abraham. He is still a shield and an exceedingly great reward to those who will go and dwell in the place of His choosing!

If God has said to you, "There's a place I want you to be", then nothing else in this world is going to satisfy you except getting up and going to that place.

You have got to say goodbye to all the people and things that would hold you back including your own thoughts and fears. God would not lead you into something worse. He has something bigger and better. He has a place of specific associations and purposes.

You will not grow and flourish anywhere else like you will in the place of God's choosing. You will not be blessed or prosper anywhere else like you will in the place God has chosen for you.

SAFE MAY NOT NECESSARILY BE SAFE

The question we all must come face to face with is; are we going to get up and obey God? Or are we going to play it safe and just stay where we are? In light of this let's remember, often what man considers being safe and secure is not necessarily safe and secure.

Yes we can go on with our Christian life outside of God's will, but our life will not be what it could be. In every believers life there must come a time when we say to God, "God, I will leave everything, I will leave whatever is necessary and obey you. I will go where you want me to go".

This brings to mind a story I heard about a young man who had gotten saved, filled with the Spirit, was actively involved in his church and on fire for God. One day while praying the Lord spoke to him and said, "I want you to go to China." Well, the young man told the Lord that he didn't want to go to China, but every time he prayed the Lord would talk to him about going to China. After awhile the young man just quit praying, because he didn't want to go to China and was tired of hearing about it. The young man ended up leaving church, and in drifting away from God found himself in trouble. After realizing the error of his way, he got his heart right with God and got back into church. He started praying again and it wasn't long before the Lord began talking about China again. The young man told the Lord he didn't want to go to China, but every time he prayed the Lord would bring up China. Well this went on for quite some time and finally one day the young man give in. He said, "OK Lord, if you want me to go to China I will go to China." The Lord then answered the young man and said, "I don't want you to go to China, I only wanted you to be willing to go".

Perhaps you are finding yourself in a similar situation as this young man regarding something the Lord is telling you. Well, it maybe that the Lord does want you to actually GO. But on the other hand, perhaps He is just wants you to be willing to GO.

If you know God has spoken to you about a particular place He wants you to be, just do the two things the Bible tells us to do; 1) Proverbs 3:5-6—Trust in the Lord with all your heart and lean not on your own understanding: In all your ways acknowledge

Him and he will direct your paths. 2) Hebrews 12:1-2. Lay aside the things that would hold you back and run with patience the race that God has set before you, looking not unto man or ourselves but unto Jesus the author and finisher of our faith.

GO, and do what you were created to do. You do not have to know how it's going to all work out. You do not have to try and figure out all the details. All you have to do is say, "Yes, here am I, Lord, send me." Once you make this commitment and step out in faith, God will go before you and make the way.

God is calling, and He will not set you in a place where His grace won't make provision and sustain you. Now understand, there is the timing of God that must be taken into consideration. But when God has said GO, it is time to GO!

So now perhaps you have a better understanding as to why we go? There are times I wish I could in some way just pour into people the same captivating power that the call of God has on my own life. I say this because even though you try your best to explain to people and bring them to an understanding regarding these things, they still will look at you and say, "I don't understand."

We go because it is the place of God's choosing. It is where His perfect will can be worked out in every area of our lives and ministries. It is a blessed place and a place where our joy is truly full. It is the place of our rewards and blessings both temporal and eternal.

CHAPTER 13

No Turning Back

Luke 9:23

If any man will come after me, let him deny himself and take up his cross daily and follow me

For decades I heard Luke 9:23 taught and preached but never had I grasped the gravity or the magnitude of these words that came from the lips of Jesus.

There is a chorus we used to sing in youth group that went like this; "I have decided to follow Jesus, I have decided to follow Jesus, I have decided to follow Jesus, no turning back, no turning back".

After I had made the decision to follow God's plan for my life and said yes to the call of God, the Lord appeared to me and spoke to me concerning my decision to follow Him.

It was early morning, my wife had already left for her job and I was sitting on our sofa doing my daily devotions. As I was meditating on the Word and praying I suddenly found myself in another place. I was no longer in our living room but found myself walking through an open field and on my left side was Jesus walking right alongside me. This visitation is forever engrained in my heart and mind, I remember every detail.

As we walked along talking, we came to a very high hill where we stopped to watch a woman who was running up to the top of the hill. As she reached the top, she turned around and looked back toward the way she came. At that moment Jesus raised his right arm, pointed at the woman and said to me, "Remember Lot's wife and don't look back!" Immediately after Jesus said this, the vision was over and I was back in our living room sitting on our sofa with my Bible in my hands praying.

Never before had I experienced such an encounter and at this point in time I was completely ignorant of such things. I knew the story of Lot's wife. I knew where it was in the Bible and even reread the story after the vision. I spent a couple of days of contemplating on the vision trying to rationalize this experience and figure out what the significance of it was where I was concerned. I began to question the

Lord about the vision and He took me directly to his Word—Luke 9:62 . . . *"No man, having put his hand to the plow and looking back is fit for the kingdom of God"*.

Something Brother Kenneth Hagin told us in Bible school concerning visions and dreams is that the Lord will at times reveal things to us in more dramatic ways, such as a vision, in order to make a lasting impression upon us because He knows that in his plans for us there will be hard challenging times ahead. Oh! How true this has proved to be.

There have been numerous occasions of deciding shall I go on or shall I just quit. Many times in the midst of despair, discouragement and frustration I wanted to give up. But this vision would rise up inside of me and I would hear the words of Jesus, "Remember Lot's wife and don't look back". And then Luke 9:62 would come to mind, "No man, having put his hand to the plow and looking back is fit for the kingdom of God". As these rose up in me, a fear of the Lord would come upon me. Not a fear that God would strike me dead or do something bad to me if I gave up and quit. No, it was a fear of disappointing my Father in heaven, a fear of becoming useless to Him. It was from these words that grace, strength, and tenacity would rise up to keep me keeping on in the plan of God.

When Jesus said, "If any man will come after me, let him deny himself and take up his cross daily and follow me", He was speaking about our being of use to Him here on the earth.

To deny oneself and follow Jesus means giving up all rights of self no matter how loud the flesh or natural human reasoning may be screaming "stop the train and let me off"! Denying yourself, that is your flesh, and following Jesus means there is only one path to walk and that's the path Jesus chooses to lead you down.

Your path may be different than mine, but each is the path Jesus has chosen and it is the only path where we can be of any value to Him. Any other path off the leading of the Lord means I will become what Jesus calls an unprofitable servant, which in the end is not a good thing.

I didn't really understand the tremendous weight of these words until I had stepped out to obey God. It's all about abandoning the "me, me, me" attitudes and desires. It involves forsaking any individual independence from the will of God and sanctifying myself totally to the Lordship of Jesus Christ. Apostle Paul calls it being a "bondservant" of Jesus Christ.

In my own experience I realize that God will allow you to be a little bit selfish when you first start out. But the further He leads you into His purposes the more he requires you to let go of yourself. Jesus brings out this truth in John 15:2. There must be a severing of those things which would hinder God from perfecting those things concerning us. There must be a purging of things that keep us out of his perfect will and hold us only in His good or permissive will. There are things God permits but they are not His perfect will.

Sometimes this severing is uncomfortable and even painful. There have been times when I have been asked to minister somewhere or visit someone and I really didn't want to because I wanted time for myself, it was inconvenient for "me". It took awhile, but the Lord finally got it home to me that He doesn't give me rules. He wants my obedience but never insists on it. He makes His will known concerning what I ought to do but He never forces me to do it. He doesn't insist on me obeying because He doesn't want obedience that is motivated by a sense of duty. He wants obedience that is motivated by love.

Obedience that is performed out of a sense of duty carries no blessing and doesn't bring glory or pleasure to God. So when occasions arise when I really don't want to do something because my flesh is insisting on self gratification, I must crucify my flesh no matter how uncomfortable it may be and say, "OK Lord, I love you therefore I will go, I will do it willingly and heartily unto you". And when I do this, I always find great blessing in the end.

God, in speaking to the Israelites in Deuteronomy 28:47 implied that there is a curse on those who don't serve Him with joyfulness and gladness of heart. Well, I don't want a curse following me around, so with joyfulness and gladness of heart I will do whatever is required of me.

There is the sanctifying work of the Holy Spirit as He works out and perfects those things concerning me. But that sanctifying work of the Holy Spirit can only take place as I sanctify myself to the will of God.

This is by no means a lesson on sanctification, but the words of Jesus in Luke 9:23 have to do with me sanctifying myself to His will. Sanctification simply means "separation, consecration, dedication, a setting apart".

When I speak about sanctifying myself, I am talking about yielding my entire being to the will of God. It means fully surrendering to God and separating myself from anything that would hinder

God from accomplishing His work in and through me. Many are waiting for God to either force or woo them into taking up their cross and following Him but that is not the way it works.

Taking up our cross and following Jesus is simply knowing what you are supposed to do and sanctifying or setting yourself apart, dedicating and consecrating yourself whole heartedly to that purpose. No one can do this for you, you must do it yourself. God will lead you right up to threshold of His purpose for you but He will not push you through it.

We see this very thing in the life of Jesus when it came to submitting to the will of God and the Cross. In John 17:19, Jesus sanctified himself for the sake of others which includes you and I. Jesus had to submit himself to the will of his Father. The Bible makes it very clear that God himself could not push Jesus to the Cross.

We must understand that Jesus took on the form of man. He became a man subject to the same weaknesses and temptations as we. In the Garden of Gethsemane we see him in agony and praying that perhaps somehow God would find some other way to procure salvation for man and the cup he was given might pass from him. Hebrews 5:7 tells us that it was with strong crying and tears that Jesus offered up prayers and supplications to Him who was able to save him from death. But in the end it was, "Father, not my will, but your will be done". Jesus humbled himself and became obedient unto death, even the death of the cross.

In Matthew 26:53-54 concerning the arrest and eventual crucifixion of Jesus, He said it was within his power to call more than twelve legions of angels to deliver him. Jesus' sanctification to the will of God was not for himself but for the sake of others. It was out of his love to do his Fathers will that he allowed himself to be taken and crucified for our sake and become the Redeemer of all mankind.

Apostle Paul tells us that we are to have this same mind set, this same attitude that Jesus had *(Philippians 2:5)*. There is a price to pay for this kind of mind set; it's the man called "self". But there is an even greater blessing and reward that can only be experienced as we forsake all and in loving obedience do the Fathers will.

2 Timothy 2:20-21
But in a great house there are not only vessels of gold and of silver, but also of wood and of earth; and some to honor, and some to

dishonor. If a man therefore purge himself from these, he shall be a vessel unto honor, sanctified, and meet for the masters use, and prepared for every good work.

This passage of scripture is speaking of sanctification. Becoming a vessel of honor prepared for the Masters use is not all up to God. There is the man side which involves us laying aside every weight and the sin that does so easily beset us and running with patience the race that is set before us, looking unto Jesus the author and finisher of our faith *(Hebrews 12:1-2).*

This process of sanctifying ourselves to the will of God is not only for our personal spiritual development, but also so that God can freely use us for the benefit of others just as He did His Son Jesus.

The process of sanctifying oneself to the will of God is not an overnight thing. With every new step in pursuing the will of God, there is some sanctifying that needs to be done. Sometimes it seems as if the price is far too great, but as someone once so eloquently put it in speaking of their own life, "The price is not greater than God's grace".

During Jesus' temptation in the Garden of Gethsemane, the Bible says that angels came and ministered to him. I am so glad that in the midst of yielding to the will of God we are not alone. Because Jesus himself experienced the same temptations concerning yielding to the will of God, He understands perfectly what we are going through in giving everything over to the will of God. He knows how to help and deliver those who are being tempted. He cannot make the decision for us, but He is always standing by, ready to help us and strengthen us when we are tempted to give up.

I remember the day we were taken to the airport for our first flight to Russia. Up until that time there was never any doubt or fear. But as we loaded our luggage into the car and started for the airport I suddenly realized the finality of our decision. I heard a voice saying, "You've done it now, you've left the stability of your job, you have nothing, what are you going to do now"?

For a moment I picked up these words in my mind and as I did, I could feel fear beginning to descend on me. It was like someone putting a heavy blanket over you and covering you in darkness. As this fear was trying to take hold of me, out of my spirit rose up the vision and words of Jesus, "Remember Lot's wife and don't look back".

The Bible says that when the enemy comes in like a flood the Spirit of the Lord will raise up a standard against him. Thank God we are not alone in our pursuit of the will of God and we can courageously push onward.

Yes there are things we have left behind for the sake of the Gospel. Even where ministry is concerned I have learned that there are times and seasons which require leaving places, things, and people behind. Our ministry in Russia was a blessed time and was the perfect will of God, but the time came when we had to leave that segment of our ministry.

Leaving was extremely hard but we cannot look back at what we had there. We must always look forward to what God has set before us. We have wonderful memories of Russia and will always cherish them, but we can't be looking back and longing for what was, even if it was a good thing.

The story of Lot's wife, along with Jesus' remarks in Luke 9:62 reveals a very sobering fact concerning following Jesus Christ. Being a disciple of Christ is not a frivolous matter!

My wife and I are currently working in Thailand, making new friends and developing new relationships. If the time comes when God says move, yes it will be hard, but we will go forward with God.

NO TURNING BACK!

CHAPTER 14

Closing Comments

I don't know, and don't even try to understand all that is involved with God's methods and timing in certain matters. I can only concur with His Word which says, "To everything there is a season, and a time to every purpose under heaven" *(Ecc.3:1)*, and that "My times are in his hand" *(Ps.31:15);* and as it say's in the book of Esther, "who knows whether you have come to the kingdom for such a time as this?" *(Esther 4:14).*

I no longer dwell on the "what could have been" of the past but have determined to rest in that God's timing is perfect and I have come into the purposes of God for such a time as this.

Many of the pages of this book were filled with tears as I wrote them. These things are close to my heart and still tender as if it were just yesterday. This is far from a complete expository of what I have experienced or of what God has done in and through me as I travel this adventurous journey in the will of God.

Being captured by the Holy Calling of God is not being chained or pulled into the will of God apart from my will. Neither is it being shackled and driven by the whip of a task master.

It is God's love for me and my love for Him that compels me to take upon myself God given tasks for the purpose of fulfilling God given purposes. It is that same love that compels me to both will and to do that which pleases Him.

Webster's Dictionary gives an illustration of what being captured involves. Webster's says, *"The absorption of a particle by an atomic nucleus; esp., the absorption of a neutron or an orbital electron that often results in the immediate emission of radiation".*

What a wonderful picture we have of the love of God—"ABSORPTION and EMISSION". The love of God absorbs us resulting in immediate emissions of God's love. Jeremiah 31:3 says the Lord loves us with an everlasting love and with loving-kindness draws us.

It is God's love for me that has absorbed me. It is His love for me that has apprehended, overtaken, and captured me. It is His love for me that binds me to His will. As a result, that love emits from my very being and allows God to accomplish His will in and through my life.

As we journey through this life, God will reveal some of the most outstanding things to us. We will hear precious and wonderful words proceed from His mouth. But at the end of our life when we stand before our Lord, the most spectacular thing we could ever behold is the smile on His face, and to hear Him say the sweetest most wonderful words we could ever hear—"WELL DONE THOU GOOD AND FAITHFUL SERVANT!"

Although there have been many challenging times, I have never once regretted letting God touch me with His power and capture me with His Holy Calling.

LET GOD TOUCH YOU WITH HIS POWER AND CAPTURE YOU WITH HIS HOLY CALLING!